Our Oswego

Memories of Growing Up & Growing Old in the Port City of Central New York

By Mike McCrobie

Illustrated by Melissa (Francisco) Martin

On the Cover:

The 1968 Seaway Supply Little League team (top). Bottom (left to right), my grandfather, Jim Fern, aboard his classic Criss-Craft on Lake Ontario; The storefront of Aero Sporting Goods on West First Street; The Hot Stove Association float in the Independence Day Parade, circa 1956; Giving my brother a bike ride in the summer of 1964.

The back cover features legendary Oswego High School coach Dave Powers as he was honored on Dave Powers Day in 1976.

Cover Design by Mallory Kelly, Step One Creative

ISBN: 1500512699
ISBN-13: 978-1500512699

DEDICATION

To my parents, Mike and Mary, and to every friend, relative, coach, teacher, classmate, neighbor, politician, store owner, co-worker and Oswegonian who made growing up in our Oswego such a memorable experience.

Table of Contents

I. Boys Will Be Boys

19 Cents Worth of Fun, Memories 15

Gigs Filled Our Need for Speed 17

Let's Go Fly a Kite 20

No Roasting These Chestnuts..22

Piano Man...24

Sandlot Ball Only a Distant Memory 27

Escaping with a Victory 29

II. Special Days, Special Memories

A Father's Day Shirt Tale..35

The Wishbook Now a Memory Book...............................37

An Earth Day Lesson...40

Not the Usual 'Treat' 42

Everyone Old Enough Recalls 11/23/63 44

The Teacher Didn't Have Any Answers 46

A Fair Day? No, a Great Day! 49

III.   Port City People

Santa Lived on East Seneca Street 55

Local Barbers Were a Cut Above................................57

A Cup of Coffee with a Childhood Idol 60

More Than Just Our Weatherman 62

The Old Guard Tradition 65

IV.   Our Town

Where were You Every April 1? 71

Christmas Shopping Circa 1973 74

Our Pay Phone 77

Sunday Ritual 79

It Suits Me to a 'T' 82

The Stamp of Approval 84

The Spirits of Breitbeck................................87

We All Scream for Ice Cream 90

The Neighborhood Store 92

Playgrounds Were Dangerous and Fun! 95

Hijinks at Hollis................................98

Backyard Carnivals................................100

The Railroad Bridge Incident 102

V.   School Days

Did You Hear They Stole the Regents?..........................109

The Handwriting's on the Wall—or is it? 111

Second to Nun 114

Did You Remember your Lunch Box?...........................115

Getting Our Kicks...118

VI.   Rockets, Trains, Automobiles & Bikes!

Remembering Rail City 123

You Always Remember Your First—Car 125

3-2-1. Ignition. Blastoff..128

Come Along for the Ride..131

VII.   Beyond Oswego

A Quazy Visitor from Outer Space 137

Say It Ain't So, Joe..139

True Colors Come Shining Through 141

The Baseball/Radio Connection 144

Happy Birthday Blockhead 146

ACKNOWLEDGMENTS

It is said that it takes a community to raise a child. So too was the case with this book. It has taken not only a community, but a lifetime of community memories to bring it to print.

In acknowledging people who made this project a reality, I run the risk of omitting key contributors. I apologize, in advance, to anyone I have neglected to thank for their assistance or encouragement.

First, to my buddies from our first ward neighborhood who provided so many of the memories of which I write. Thanks to Rich Burger; Joe Losurdo; Johnny and David Muldoon; Donnie, Timmy and Billy (Bit) Curro; Randy Vincent; Tim (Nimmer) Dufore; Dave Smith; Mike Wapen; my brother Jeff, and all the kids who made our wonder years so wonder-ful. Likewise, to my high school friends, too numerous to name. Only a small fraction of our escapades can actually be printed!

To my friend and colleague Melissa (Francisco) Martin whose illustrations adorn these pages. When I was seeking an illustrator, Melissa volunteered before I even asked for her assistance. Her drawings, reminiscent of the "Dick & Jane" basal reading books of our youth, capture the reflective nature of the writings.

I also extend a profound thank you to my former student Shane Stepien, owner of Step One Creative. I can't believe that it has been over twenty-five years since young Shane Stepien was in my high school journalism class. I take great pride in his professional accomplishments, and I am honored that his public relations firm (and another former student, graphic artist Mallory Kelly) created the cover for this book.

I thank Mike Brown, former director of printing services for the Oswego City School District, for his publishing and design expertise, in addition to his friendship.

Don Kranz has been Oswego's photographer for most of my life. Whether shooting supermodifieds at the Oswego Speedway, candid pictures around town, or team photos of hundreds of Little League teams over the years, Don was omnipresent. It didn't surprise me a bit when, approached out of the blue this summer, Don provided a treasure trove of photos—several of which appear in these pages.

I appreciate the assistance of my friend Jim Farfaglia. Jim's "encore career" is writing, and his guidance throughout the self-publishing process has been invaluable.

An enormous debt of gratitude to Bill Reilly of the river's end bookstore, who not only offered me advice with this project, but who continues to promote literacy to Oswegonians young and old.

To Sarah McCrobie, Jon Spaulding, Andrew Poole, and Colleen Goewey of the *Palladium-Times* for getting me into this mess, by allotting me space twice a month to publish the columns that eventually became this book.

I offer sincere gratitude to every teacher of writing I ever had, and to my former colleagues in the English Departments at both Hannibal and Oswego High Schools. These professionals not only shaped my career, but my personal life as well.

To my wife Sally with whom I have grown up and hope to grow old here in our Oswego. And to my four children, Matthew, Sarah, Brian, and Eric who suffered the difficulties of being a "teacher's kid" during their school years, not to mention having to endure a lifetime of "Dad Jokes."

Finally, to my ancestors, who had the good sense to put down roots in Oswego, New York. Our Oswego really has been a great place to live.

Foreword

I retired in June of 2012 after a 33 year career teaching high school English and journalism. Two months into retirement, I realized that I wasn't very good at it. I needed something—anything—to do. One of the first things I considered was fulfilling a lifelong ambition to be a newspaperman. Luckily, at the time, my daughter was the editor at the Oswego daily, the *Palladium-Times*. Though she made me submit some samples of my writing as if I were a stranger off the street, she reluctantly granted me the title of community columnist, and allowed me 800 words twice a month.

Don't get me wrong; I have no regrets about my career in education. In fact, I loved being a teacher, but when I was a seventeen-year-old high school senior in the fall of 1974, I took a journalism elective from Mr. Charlie Loschiavo and caught the journalism bug. Back then, I figured that by age 55 I'd either be the next Woodward or Bernstein of Watergate fame, or have a weekly byline in *Sports Illustrated*. Well, this certainly isn't *Sports Illustrated*, but it is compilation of some of the columns I have written over the last two years for the *Palladium-Times*.

At first, I didn't know what I was getting myself into. I wasn't sure what I would find to write about, but I knew I wouldn't waste my twice-monthly newspaper space on politics or negativity. There's enough of that around. I settled on a simple recipe for my writing—two spoonfuls of nostalgia, a cup of Oswego history, one part grumpy old man, and a pinch of humor.

As a novice retiree, I've found myself reminiscing a lot. My recollections of the Oswego of my childhood provided plenty to write about. I've written about everything from intriguing people (my childhood friends) to inanimate objects (19 cent plastic cars, and a special pay phone, to name just two).

In publishing this book, I feel like a man facing a firing squad.

There are hundreds—no, thousands—of my former students out there who would love to catch me misspelling a word, writing a run-on sentence or omitting an apostrophe. After 33 years of using a red pen on their essays and compositions, I'm putting my work out there. I guess turnabout is fair play and I welcome constructive criticism.

After writing over fifty bi-monthly columns, this book is a result of positive feedback from readers. Sure, many people have a bucket list that contains "write a book," but the idea never crossed my mind until people began stopping me on the street, calling my home, and e-mailing me with words of encouragement. One day, an elderly woman left an answering machine message complimenting a column. The last thing she said before hanging up was, "You should put these stories into a book." So I'm taking her advice and giving it a try.

The title of my newspaper column is *My Oswego*. I kicked around several ideas for the column sig that accompanies each piece. I considered *Positively Oswego*, because of my intent to be upbeat about my hometown. I also considered *Our Town*, but it wouldn't be fair to be compared to Thornton Wilder's classic play of the same name. I settled on *My Oswego*. It comes from the fact that I like Oswego. I'm an "Oswego guy." I was born here, educated here, worked and raised my family here, and I'll probably die here (though I hope the latter isn't anytime in the immediate future).

But I realized as I was choosing the pieces for this book, the nostalgic observations and fond memories that follow are not mine alone, but ours. So *My Oswego* has become *Our Oswego*.

I hope you enjoy *Our Oswego*.

1

BOYS WILL BE BOYS

Mike McCrobie

19 Cents Worth of Fun, Memories

(June 25, 2014)

You can't get much for a quarter nowadays, but when it comes to childhood toy memories, one of my favorites cost less than a quarter—nineteen cents to be exact.

Ask any Oswego boy of the 1960s what a "19 cent-er" was, and he will likely smile and recall a story something like this . . .

My buddies and I would head downtown with a buck in our pockets, with our final destination being the toy department in the basement level of Green's five-and-ten store. Our purchases on summer days were not the board games that we would put on our Christmas lists months later like Hands Down or Operation. Instead, we sought out simple, plastic cars. These cars were less than six inches long, and were neither fancy nor motorized. They were plain, one-color cars that cost a mere 19 cents. They were primitive by today's toy standards, at least until we got them home and began a makeover.

Once home, our task was simple—turn these nondescript plastic cars into racing machines that resembled the cars of our idols at the Oswego Speedway.

Unlike the pre-packaged, hard plastic model car kits that came with instructions, we had no templates, no accessories, and no assembly illustrations. What we did have was our imaginations, and on a good day, maybe a picture of the Oswego Speedway supermodifieds, taken by Don Kranz for the *Oswego Eagle*—the official race-night program at the "Home of Champions."

How we began our conversion of these simple toy cars was a lesson in good old-fashioned boyhood ingenuity. We would take the basic design (all of these plastic cars were identical—only the colors varied) and we'd fashion tail fins, spoilers, and front ends mostly out of cardboard. For me, the best source of materials was mom's closet, where I would borrow shoe boxes to cut into pieces. Dad's dresser provided pipe cleaners that served as roof supports or roll cages for our creations.

15

Add some Testors glue (man, that stuff smelled good) and a couple tiny jars of model car paint, and the transformation was underway.

I'm not sure how my buddies David Muldoon, Billy Curro, Rich Burger and I decided who would build which of our favorite drivers' cars, but I don't ever recall us fighting over it. There were plenty of Oswego Speedway idols with cool cars, great paint schemes, and neat nicknames to go around. Whether we built Bentley Warren's L'il Deuce or the 10 Pins of Nolan Swift; Jimmy Shampine's famed 8-ball, or the 40 of Stormin' Norman Mackereth, we spent hours creating these replica cars to race.

Somehow, through patience and trial-and-error, the simple 19-cent cars that we purchased in the morning, would be ready for a full card of late afternoon racing down a piece of plywood or even an elevated ironing board on someone's porch or sloped driveway.

The guys in my neighborhood competed at everything, and racing our 19 cent cars was no exception. My cars rarely, if ever, won a race. Whether we were racing for speed or for total distance, I couldn't figure out why I kept losing. I assumed it was just because I was never mechanically inclined. Logic told me that all the cars were basically the same. No matter what accessories we added or what colors we painted them, my buddies' cars shouldn't have been that much faster than mine. How naïve I was!

After each race, we'd retrieve our cars, head back to the starting line at the top of the ramp, and run another heat. One day, I picked up my friend Richard's car to return it to him. I noticed his car was a lot heavier than mine. I couldn't understand why his was heavier, or how a heavier car would go faster than a lighter one. Richard explained the physics behind it, and showed me that he had jammed clay, for weight, into every nook and cranny in the underside of his car to leave the competition in the dust. It worked. Then, he revealed the real "look behind the curtain" secret. He said for even more weight, he'd take a sinker from his fishing tackle box and wedge it tightly in the undercarriage before packing in the clay. Genius!

We'd race for hours, rewriting our record books with faster speeds and greater distances with each "pit stop" and subsequent trip down the ramp. I guess looking back, those records should have an asterisk (*) next to them because of the performance-enhancing substances that we put into the cars for weight.

The price of our "19-cent-ers" rose to 29 cents by the time we became teenagers and outgrew this pastime—a lesson in economics for us kids. I actually saw one on eBay sell for $10.99 recently. It had the original 19 cent price sticker on it. More inflation.

Though these cars cost only 19 cents, there was no putting a price tag on the hours of play they inspired back then, and on the fond memories they bring back today.

•

'Gigs' Filled Our Need for Speed
(August 6, 2013)

I don't know about *all* kids of the '60s and '70s, but my friends and I did lots of "hands-on" things that many kids of today's video game generation do not even leave the couch for. We played every sport known to man, but one of the more challenging things we did was build gigs.

Not everybody called them gigs. Depending on which Oswego neighborhood you grew up in, they might have been labeled "carts," "buggies," "soap-box racers," "go-carts," or some combination of the above names, but we spent hours designing, constructing, and racing our own cars in hopes of becoming the next Nolan Swift, Jim Shampine, or Norm Mackereth.

The contraptions we built were as varied as the names they were called. Yes, I said, *we built*—not *dad built*. Give a kid in this day-and-age a project to build a homemade motorless go-cart, and the first thing he or she will do is look for plans on the Internet. The second thing the millennial kid will likely do is tell mom or dad to build it for him! Back in the day, we did it by trial-and-error. There were many trials, and lots of errors, but the life lessons we learned were priceless. We learned to create and plan, improvise and re-evaluate.

There were no Henry Fords in my neighborhood, but it didn't prevent us from building gigs anyway. The driveway was our assembly line. I don't ever remember buying supplies to build a gig, but I remember lots of scavenger hunts looking for materials. (Have you ever tried carrying a half-sheet of plywood six blocks on a Stingray bicycle?) We scoured the neighborhood from construction sites to our parents' garages for plywood for the seat, splintered two-by-fours for the chassis, and some type of rebar or metal for the axels. The tow rope and the wheels were easiest to locate, but after my friends and I searched the first ward for these supplies, I know for a fact there were some downed clotheslines and some baby carriages, shopping carts, and lawn mowers with missing wheels. Once the materials were gathered, our vehicles were assembled and held together by nails that we either "borrowed" from coffee cans in our dad's workshop, or crooked nails that we had to straighten out by pounding with a hammer on the sidewalk. (Many times, the hammer found a left thumb, instead of the nail that needed straightening, but like I said, trial and error!)

Everyone knows that the Carusos are Oswego's first family of racing. The Caruso boys weren't just the next generation proprietors of the Oswego Speedway, but as kids, they were movers and shakers on the Oswego gig racing scene. I spoke with Doug Caruso a while back about gig racing. Doug's face lit up as he recalled building his car by day and racing it on warm summer nights, with his best friends being his fiercest competitors.

My dad was the city recreation director and I distinctly remember a young Romey Caruso constantly calling the house asking dad to help sanction gig racing. According to an article that appeared in the *Palladium Times* on March 11, 1969, a group presented petitions "signed by 1,316 adults and 705 children" at a common council meeting seeking the support of city fathers for gig racing. The article, written by Don McCann, stated that the request was tentatively approved to set aside eleven city streets, three times a week for gig racing. Romey's persistence paid off.

Gig racing courses wound through every Oswego neighborhood. In my neighborhood, the green flag dropped at the corner of Ontario and West Van Buren Streets. We coasted north down Ontario Street towards where Crisafulli Park now stands, where we would take a sharp left onto Bronson Street (heading west). Since we rarely built a gig with a brake, we were usually stopped by the chain-link fence on Liberty Street that surrounds the steam station. The gigs were obviously not equipped with air bags either, so those stops were quite sudden.

The city provided barricades, but we supplied the fun. There were some mishaps such as lost wheels and the occasional rollover resulting in some nasty road rash, but everyone survived the setbacks, and as the unwritten rule of the '60s stated, we finished our nightly sessions and headed home when the street lights came on, or when dad whistled from the porch—whichever came first.

As we kids of the '60s became teenagers of the '70s, and our gigs were replaced by drivers' licenses and real cars, downhill racing was kept alive by the Oswego Jaycees. This civic organization, most widely known for its tireless efforts producing the Independence Day parade, also sponsored and supervised annual city-wide gig races at the end of the summer on the hill near Fitzhugh Park School.

So, when I hear kids talking about video games like *Grand Theft Auto*, *Gran Turismo*, or *Need for Speed*, I just shake my head and recall how we kids of the '60s fulfilled our need for speed by racing gigs.

•

Let's Go Fly a Kite
(May 29, 2013)

I can only wonder what kids of today will recall when they reminisce about their "good old days." I fear that the electronic video game age has made some of life's simple pleasures obsolete. Will today's kids have fond recollections of experiences, and begin sentences with "Remember the time when we . . . ." or will their formative years be just a blur of video game dungeons and battles fought on 55 inch HD televisions?

Oh well, I guess that'll be their problem.

For me, Oswego is a great place on a great lake. I was fortunate enough throughout my college years to have a summer job in one of the best places in town—Breitbeck Park. It wasn't a glamorous job, but when my friends were sweating out their summer jobs in one of our now-closed local factories like Hammermill, Breneman, or Columbia Mills, I was my own boss on the south shore of Lake Ontario for eight hours a day as a city laborer at Breitbeck Park. Talk about a "room with a view!"

No matter how hot our July and August days get, there is usually a breeze at Breitbeck. One summer day, in 1979, I had most of my morning work done when the traveling activities director for the summer recreation program arrived. It was Jack Pidgeon. Jack, of course, was a long-time sixth grade teacher at Riley School, but each summer, he went from playground to playground to supervise kids' activities such as archery and golf.

The particular day that I recall was very windy. Both the archery arrows and the wiffle golf balls were flailing like butterflies in the stiff wind. With his usual activities scrapped, Jack jokingly said, "The only thing today would be good for is flying a kite." One thing led to another, and after a quick trip downtown to Green's Department store, Jack returned with a couple kites and the biggest ball of string I had ever seen.

Jack gave a quick lesson to the neighborhood kids on kite building (once a teacher, always a teacher) and I contributed a long piece of bed sheet for the kite's tail that had actually been my drop cloth when I was painting that morning. After the kids did a formal countdown, we were ready for launch.

Jack must have channeled his inner science teacher to create the kite of all kites. With gusty winds out of the west, the launch team (consisting of the 8-10 kids who hung out at the park everyday) headed to the east end of Breitbeck, overlooking Wright's Landing. As soon as we let go of the kite, it climbed faster and further than any kite I had ever seen. NASA would've been proud, because this kite was a flying machine. Sandwiched between the Apollo program of the '60s and the space shuttles of the '80s was our kite mission of the summer of '79.

I knew we were onto something when, after about twenty minutes of releasing string, Jack went to his car to get binoculars to maintain visual contact with the mother ship. We were pretty sure we still had control of the kite, but we lost sight of it as the string became draped over the grain elevator east of the U.S. Coast Guard station. There was so much resistance on the kite that we feared it would drag one of the neighborhood kids with it, so he and I took turns tethering the kite, while continuing to release more string.

One of the older kids, Alan Leavens, who was a playground regular by virtue of living directly across from Breitbeck on Lake Street, took it upon himself to be our "scout." He got on his bike and pedaled east to get an exact location. Alan was gone for what seemed like an eternity, and of course, this was the era long before kids carried cell phones. So when he returned and yelled, "It's on the east side; it's over the Fort!" we figured it was time to end the mission. No way were we going to reel in a couple thousand feet of kite string, so our "mission control" decided to cut its losses (and the string) and send our flying machine into the wild blue yonder.

There are a lot of important things that have happened in my life since that summer day in 1979, yet for some reason, the memories of our kite launch have lived on. Why? I wish I knew. Maybe it was the success of the mission. Maybe it was because it was such a simple pleasure on a summer day. But it was, and still is, a great memory. In fact, every once in a while, on a windy day when I run into Jack Pidgeon, I say, "Great day to fly a kite." And he smiles, because he remembers too.

•

No Roasting These Chestnuts
(December 12, 2012)

There's nothing like a nice autumn walk around Oswego before the inevitable winter hibernation officially begins.

While walking on West Albany Street this fall, I stumbled (both literally and figuratively) upon a staple of my childhood that I hadn't thought about in years—chestnuts.

Back in the '60s and '70s, in my west side neighborhood, there were dozens of chestnut trees, or as we called them, horse chestnut trees.

In addition to tackle football in the neighborhood, a rite of fall was the collection of horse chestnuts. Our gang from the neighborhood that consisted of several Curros, a couple Muldoons, a pair of McCrobies, a Losurdo and a Burger, was not a patient bunch. We often couldn't wait for Mother Nature to drop the chestnuts from the trees encased in their thorny green shells. No, we had to speed along the harvest by getting the chestnuts to the ground with some assistance.

What we lacked in patience, we more than made up for in resourcefulness. The real daredevils climbed the trees with a boost or human ladder from the rest of us, to shake the limbs and free our booty. Next, we'd resort to weaponry. Since most of us had just finished playing over a thousand games of summer sandlot baseball, our arms were in good enough shape to throw everything from garbage can lids (back then, of course, they were made of metal, not plastic) to footballs into the trees. It wasn't a very good trade-off, however, when three chestnuts fell to the ground, but our football became wedged in the crotch of a tree.

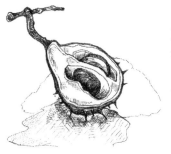

Being the least adventurous of the kids in the neighborhood, my preferred method of extraction was not throwing or climbing, but beating the chestnuts out of the tree with a pole.

My parents maintained Sylvan Glen Apartments at the time, so I just happened to know where to get my hands on a 24-foot extension pole that was used for washing windows (when it wasn't harvesting chestnuts out of trees).

Needless to say, by using these three methods, the boys in the neighborhood usually ended up with bushel baskets full of chestnuts by the time the snow flew.

Back then, leaf-burning was allowed in the city limits, so when dad took his Zippo lighter and torched the freshly raked leaves in front of our house, the popping sound made by a handful of chestnuts would be the autumn equivalent of an exploding pack of firecrackers.

In a Norman Rockwell setting, the remaining chestnuts would be roasting on an open fire on Thanksgiving or Christmas. But the guys I grew up with didn't come out of a Rockwell painting. In our mischievous plan, we took our bushel baskets and brown paper grocery bags from the A & P full of chestnuts, and squirreled them away until the first snowfall.

As luck would have it, quite often the first snow was of the heavy, wet variety. The "good packin,'" as we called it, made for some great snowball fights in the Bronson Street woods. But what made those first-of-the-season snowballs lethal, were the chestnuts that we packed into the middle of each one, like the candy center in a Tootsie Roll Pop. The recipe was simple. Take one chestnut, grab two handfuls of wet snow, and pack a sphere suitable for throwing.

Though it's been decades since I was hit by one, I vividly remember how much they stung when I got hit by them. They also made loud, echoing noises when an errant throw occasionally (but accidentally, of course) struck a passing car. I often wonder how we never lost an eye, chipped a tooth, or suffered a concussion at the hands of these projectiles.

Walking around town recently, and stumbling across one of the few remaining chestnut trees, I couldn't help but reminisce about all of the chestnut trees that provided so much ammunition for mischievous kids in our Oswego back in the day.

•

Piano Man
(May 14, 2014)

Some of my greatest memories of sports come from my four years playing Little League baseball in Oswego. My team, Seaway Supply, sponsored by the local plumbing and heating supplier on West First Street, only needed five new players in 1967, so I was a fifth round draft choice for the franchise.

Our manager, Lupe DiMerio, was not only an Oswego sports legend, but a close personal friend of my father (no doubt insuring that I would be chosen for his team). Lupe owned a local sports shop, Lupe's Sporting Goods (of course) on West Bridge Street, across from the hospital. The interesting thing about Lupe's was that it seemed to be the only sporting goods store that never sold anything! There were only a few old wooden baseball bats gathering dust on a bat rack and some sanitary baseball socks on the shelves that seemed to be yellowing from age. Lupe's certainly didn't rival the big box sporting goods chains of today. It was more of a coffee shop/soda fountain, a relic of days gone by when corner drug stores and soda fountains were gathering places for adults by day and teenagers by night.

Lupe was a great guy, who lived in a time before the phrase "PC" came into vogue. In fact, there were very few politically correct adult male role models in the 1960s. Building the self-esteem of young Little Leaguers wasn't a priority for coaches of that era (and I'm glad it wasn't). If you dropped a fly ball in the outfield, it was almost a certainty that you'd be pulled from the line-up at the end of the inning. (Occasionally, if it was a *key* error, your replacement would trot onto the field to replace you *on the spot*—before the inning even ended!)

Because the statute of limitations has expired, I can now admit that after my first Seaway Supply practice, I was a victim of what today would be called hazing and bullying—but I loved every minute of it. You see, Seaway Supply had an informal initiation ceremony for its new players. After the first practice each spring, all fifteen members of the team would head to Lupe's house on West Mohawk Street to get their uniforms. Before donning the gray-and-red wool suits, the rookies would be ceremoniously tossed into the "pricker" bushes in front of Lupe's house. Veteran players (my rookie year, it was Pete Reidy, Mark Roy, Paul DiMerio, and Jim Kessler among others) would grasp the newcomers' arms and legs, and swing them back-and-forth before launching them into the bushes. So, in May of 1967, instead of calling a lawyer or complaining to mom and dad after my "hazing," I smiled all the way home on my bike, with my glove on the handle bars, and my new uniform in a brown grocery bag, because I was part of something special. I had been initiated as a Little Leaguer on Seaway Supply.

Once the season started, like most nine-year-old rookies, I'd play my minimum three innings a week, get a solitary at-bat, and be thrilled just to put on the uniform and watch my older teammates like Billy and Tommy Drumm play us into the city championship game against the east side champions sponsored by Goldberg's Furniture.

My moment of glory—if you could call it that—came against our west side rivals, the Elks. I had gone hitless for the entire season, but the Elks were the cellar dwellers, so I got to play an *entire* game. After going 0-for-2 in my first two plate appearances, I knew my third at-bat would probably be my last, so I went up to plate swinging. Much to my surprise, I hit the first pitch solidly. It *felt* good. It *sounded* good. (In those days, the crack of the bat was from a wooden flame-treated Hillerich & Bradsby, not some $300 titanium alloy bat.) The hit was a solid line drive over the second baseman's head. I dropped the bat and started an all-out sprint to first base. Before I was very far out of the batter's box, the right fielder had picked up the ball on one hop and was ready to fire to first base. (You

The Piano Man
Seaway Supply, 1969

see, my "all-out" sprint wasn't much of a sprint. I was, am, and forever shall be, a slow runner.) The play at first base wasn't even close. I was out by a mile.

What I thought was the first base hit of my career, became a 9-3 (right field-to-first base) putout in the scorebook.

If that wasn't humiliating enough, on the way back to the dugout, Lupe yelled across the diamond, "Hey kid, I don't mind that you're carrying a piano on your back when you run to first, but you don't have to stop and play it on the way!" (Remember, no political correctness in the '60s.)

So, long before Billy Joel wrote the lyrics to his song of the same title, I was the "Piano Man" of my Seaway Supply Little League team.

•

Sandlot Ball Only a Distant Memory
(June 26, 2013)

I drove around town the other day looking for kids playing a sandlot baseball game. Starting at Fort Ontario, I dejectedly rode to Fitzhugh and Riley (Peglow) Parks. All I found on the ball fields, on a beautiful summer day, were empty outfields and lonely backstops. I headed west to Kingsford and Leighton. More desolation. Finally, I went to the site of my childhood sandlot—Crisafulli Park, adjacent to Breitbeck. This was the most depressing stop of all. The field was a ghost town—with overgrown baselines where no one had tried to stretch a double into a triple for many years.

Since I couldn't find a game, my only solution was to sit and reminisce about the sandlot games of bygone days. Before the city named the field after war hero Charles Crisafulli, and before there were dugouts and a concession stand, our sandlot was called the Diamond Match (after the factory that had once employed hundreds of Oswegonians making stick matches nearby).

What was special about our sandlot? Everything. The camaraderie, the competition, the never-ending game, in which the first pitch was thrown in late June and the final out tallied on Labor Day. Some of my most vivid childhood memories took place on that dusty piece of real estate at the corner of Lake and Ontario Streets.

Just like Scott Smalls, Squints, Hamilton Porter, and Benny "The Jet" Rodriguez in the 1993 movie *The Sandlot*, I flashed back to my friends, doing what we did hundreds of times—play baseball, for the love of the game. I recalled Tim "Nimmer" Dufore, a wicked pull-hitter, launching foul balls off the picture window of the Sweetings' house on the corner of Bronson and Ontario. I saw David Muldoon, a left-handed hitter coming to the plate, and the outfielders complaining about shifting to right and center fields, because the opposite field was always foul. I pictured my friend Rich Burger powering homeruns, not only over the fence, but over Bronson Street, and into the garden in Rocco Fortino's side yard. Poor Mr. Fortino. I'm sure that some summers, he harvested more Rawlings baseballs than Hothouse tomatoes. I closed my eyes and imagined Billy "Bit" Curro doing his best Bobby Murcer imitation by reaching over the fence to rob a homerun. I remembered my pal Joe Losurdo, our steady, quiet, everyday player—our Roger Maris.

I recall two "captains"—one tossing the bat, the other catching it near the trademark, then alternating hand-over-hand, and arguing whether one had called "no tops" while the ritual of choosing teams played out.

When we couldn't muster the whole gang for a real game, we found other ways to play. Some days, it was a heated game of "flies and grounders." Other times, we'd hone our skills with a round of "infield." One of us would hit, like a coach, while everyone else took an infield position, fielded balls, and threw out imaginary runners, as if we were warming up for game seven of the World Series.

There was no greater sandlot ritual, though, than the disposal of a broken bat. We only had wooden bats back then. When they cracked, we often extended their life spans with a couple small nails and a roll of black friction tape from some unsuspecting dad's toolbox. But when the bat met its final demise, we placed it in an appropriate eternal resting place—not the landfill, but the sandlot itself. I guess we figured any bat that gave its life for us on the field, deserved a proper burial. In a rite that played out dozens of times over the years, we'd take the broken bat handle and bury it (knob up) in the dirt behind home plate by pounding it as deeply into the earth as we could, usually with another bat, which would probably suffer the same fate by summer's end. As I sat the other day, reflecting on this committal ceremony, I was tempted to conduct an archaeological dig—in hopes of unearthing the skeletal remains of my

31-inch Cleon Jones model Adirondack bat from the 1960s.

It occurred to me that one of the best things about our sandlot was that I can never remember an adult setting foot on our field. We kids organized games, settled disputes, kept score, and even administered first aid for minor cuts and bee stings without grown-ups. Parents didn't bring us water bottles (we drank from a neighbor's garden hose), we didn't sign liability waivers, and we didn't wear batting gloves, helmets, elbow guards or heart-protectors.

As I left the sandlot after an afternoon of reflection last week, the words from another great baseball movie echoed in my ears. I could hear the booming voice of James Earl Jones' character, Terrance Mann, from *Field of Dreams,* saying, "The one constant through all the years has been baseball. . . . baseball has marked the time. This field, this game: it's a part of our past. It reminds of us of all that once was good and it could be again."

Yeah, our sandlot was good; it was really good.

•

Escaping With a Victory
(April 17, 2013)

Most people don't know this, but thirty years ago, I spent some time at Auburn Prison.

Wait. Let me explain.

My men's league softball team (Ferlito's Express) had anticipated the 1983 softball season all winter long. Little did we know as we counted down to opening day, that our first game would be played behind the towering concrete walls of the maximum security Auburn Correctional Facility.

We had heard that Auburn Prison had an intramural program for its inmates, and they were looking for teams to play "from the outside." My friends Bobby Farrell, Mark Ferlito, Jamie Cullinan, Mark Lazzaro,

Gibby Thompson and I had kicked the idea around all winter and said, "Why not?"

A letter to the prison's recreation director led to a series of phone calls, and it was settled—we'd travel to Auburn for a slow pitch softball game on Sunday, April 17, 1983.

Back then, we often traveled to tournaments in our sponsor Jim Ferlito's motor home, nicknamed the "Urban Assault Vehicle" after the RV Bill Murray commandeered in the popular movie of the time, *Stripes*. We casually piled in for the forty minute ride to Auburn in much the same way we would've traveled to Nestle's Park in Fulton or Hopkins Road Fields in Liverpool for a regular tournament.

Shortly, our jovial, devil-may-care attitude changed. Some of the guys saw "it" before I did. "It" was the sixty foot high wall that surrounds Auburn Prison. Suddenly, the one question on all of our minds was, "What have we gotten ourselves into?"

From the time we checked in at the guard shack, we knew it wasn't going to be just another day at the ballpark. Our roster, mailed in advance, had to be verified by photo ID. The equipment was carefully checked by the guards for what they called "contraband." We wouldn't need our spikes, for the playing field was not the green grass of Fort Ontario, but asphalt. The field could've been a parking lot had the painted lines marked rows of parking spaces instead of baselines.

To get on the field, we had to walk past a group of inmates in the exercise yard who took a break from their weightlifting to see who, or what, we were. They made some comments that the guards told us to ignore, but it was hard to ignore the whistles and the catcalls from guys who looked like they could bench press our Winnebago!

Amazingly, once we got by the unique setting, the softball game was not much different than any other game our team played in the '80s. The captains met for ground rules at home plate, and the inmates were the home team, not by virtue of a coin toss, but because they never got to play road games.

The first play of the game set the tone for the afternoon. The leadoff hitter was a wiry little lefty. He opened the game with a double down the left field line. I was playing third base, and had no shot at the ball as it sliced over the bag (not a real base, but a white square painted on the pavement). Our left fielder, Jerry Brown, who was on the other side of the law from our opponents as a career state trooper, picked up the ball and saw that the hitter wasn't going to be satisfied with a double, but was trying to stretch it into a triple. Jerry threw a strike to me covering third, and the ball easily beat the runner. I had a split second (while waiting with the ball in my glove before attempting a tag) to wonder, "Is this guy going to shank me to get to the base?" Instead, he went into a perfect hook slide—on the asphalt—to try to avoid the tag. Instinctively, I swept the glove, catching the back of his head to make the tag. The umpire, an inmate himself, who was paid 50 cents for officiating, made the "out" call. Without argument, the runner got up off the pavement and jogged away. As he did, he looked at me and said, "Nice tag man."

The game moved very quickly without incident, though there were some oddities that we were unaccustomed to. It was strange for us to stand in the painted on-deck circle and not swing a warm-up bat, but the guard stationed on top of our dugout only let one bat out at a time. During our first ups, our on-deck batter, Gene Tracy, asked the guard why he couldn't have a bat to swing. "To you it's a warm-up bat," the guard said, "But if you leave it layin' around, it's a weapon to them."

GULP!

At the end of the game, the scoreboard, with little blue and gold New York State license-plate numbers fashioned in the prison metal shop, read Visitors 22, Home 17. The headline on the sports page of the *Palladium-Times* the following day read "Ferlito Farms Escapes Auburn Prison With Victory."

As we went through the traditional post-game handshake line, two things came to mind. First, the sincerity with which our opponents acknowledged our visit. They thanked us for playing, and invited us back any time. (We actually did go back the following spring.) And as I observed their sportsmanship and saw the appreciation in their eyes, I also realized that I was looking into the eyes and shaking the hands of convicted arsonists, rapists, and murderers.

•

2

SPECIAL DAYS, SPECIAL MEMORIES

Mike McCrobie

A Father's Day Shirt Tale

(June 12, 2013)

I look at Father's Day with mixed emotions. As a father of four grown children, Father's Day should be a day for me to be a proud dad of the family my wife and I have raised—and I certainly am.

But in a cruel twist of irony, my own father died as the sun came up on Father's Day in 1999, so as I said, it's a day of both present-day happiness and sad reflection.

My father was a middle class man who became a dad in the 1950s, a grandfather in the 1980s and lived and worked in Oswego his entire life. Born a year before the Great Depression, he never owned a Calvin Klein or Armani suit. Instead, his wardrobe was typical of the time period, of his job, and of his means. It's kind of hard to describe, but Roy Campbell "Mike" McCrobie wore nothing fancy, yet always looked good. He never heard of a tanning salon, but always seemed to have a tan. He never worked out at a gym, but was solidly built. He was neither rich man nor poor man.

It was a shirt-and-tie day for kindergarten graduation in 1963, so dad wasn't wearing the Hawaiian print shirt or the flannel plaid.

So when he passed away, 14 years ago, it struck me, while cleaning out his closets and sorting through his belongings, how few possessions he actually had. Maybe he thinned out his wardrobe as he, too, became gaunt with the multiple myeloma that eventually claimed his life on that June Sunday in 1999. But for whatever reason, there was very little cleaning I had to do.

As I sorted his clothes into boxes for the Salvation Army and bags for the trash, two items of clothing, hidden in the furthest corner of his small closet, took me to a place that I hadn't been throughout his illness, the calling hours, or the funeral.

My dad was certainly no hoarder, so finding two contrasting shirts hanging side-by-side, made me wonder why these particular items survived the test of time. One was a navy blue, plaid, flannel, long sleeve shirt. The other was a bright orange floral patterned, short sleeve Hawaiian shirt. I was in my early forties when he died, and I am positive that I had never seen dad wear either of these shirts in my lifetime.

I don't know when or why, but these two garments somehow got pushed to the dark recesses of his closet by his polyester pants of the '70s and his Arnold Palmer sweaters of the '60s.

No supernatural elements were at work here, but these two shirts seemed to speak to me about the past and about my father.

The flannel shirt was all wool—real wool—and bore the tag from a downtown men's store long since put out of business by malls and online retailers.

The Hawaiian shirt was not a knock-off or a cotton shirt with a Hawaiian print that you can get today for $20. It was 100 percent silk. Come to find out, it was sent to my father by his sister when she lived on Oahu, before Hawaii was even granted statehood in 1959.

I have no idea why these two garments moved me the way they did. Perhaps it was their own 40-year marriage next to each other on hangers in dad's closet. Maybe it was the faint scent of his Old Spice, lingering on the shirts that lured me in. Or maybe it was the strange paradox of these two garments surviving for decades, side-by-side: long sleeve/short sleeve, silk/wool, summer apparel/winter apparel, dark blue plaid/bright floral orange. Maybe it was none of these contradictions. Perhaps it was the fact that he hadn't worn these as a dying seventy-year-old, but as a young man with his entire life ahead of him, who hadn't yet dreamed of the son who would discover these treasures a half-century later.

I do know that neither the Salvation Army box nor the garbage bag for the dump was going to be a suitable resting place for these two shirts.

So, a couple times each year, on cold winter days, the woolen shirt comes out of *my* closet. Likewise, the Hawaiian shirt frequently emerges for a festive summer occasion. I wear these not because I want to make a fashion statement with vintage clothing, but because even a grown man needs to remember his dad once in a while.

Happy Father's Day.

•

The Wishbook Now a Memory Book
(December 11, 2013)

Christmas is two weeks away, so there's no better time than now to reflect on holiday traditions. We didn't have many Christmas traditions in the McCrobie household of the 1960s, but the one I recall most vividly was born on Thanksgiving. On a Thanksgiving morning in the mid '60s, while my mother was busy in the kitchen, she threw a book at my brother and me (to distract us and keep us out of her way) and said, "Here, look through this and see if there's anything you guys want for Christmas."

The book was the Sears Christmas catalog. It kept us occupied for hours that morning and a ritual was born. Every Thanksgiving, with the Macy's Parade on the TV, my brother and I would sit in the living room with pen, paper, and the Sears Wishbook. Whether we were young enough to be writing to Santa or old enough to be making a list for mom and dad, the Thanksgiving morning trip through the Sears Wishbook became tradition.

Now that I'm in the nostalgic stage of life, I went looking for a Wishbook, partly for research, but mainly just to reminisce. I chose to look for a 1968 Wishbook for a couple reasons. First, in 1968, I was 11 and my brother 8—great ages for boys and toys. And '68 was the year Sears renamed its Christmas supplement catalog, the Wishbook. I discovered that you can find a 1968 Wishbook at the Onondaga County Public Library, but you cannot buy one at Sears. Ironic. Thank goodness for eBay. I'm too embarrassed to tell how much I spent for a 1968 Sears Wishbook, but I won the online auction, and on a chilly November day a few weeks back, my 1968 Wishbook came in the mail—in much the same way as it would've been delivered 45 years ago.

When I opened the package, it was 1968 again. Through the eyes of a nostalgic adult, the Wishbook was a refreshing blast from the past. The book didn't showcase items I wanted, it resurrected the childhood I once had. I couldn't put it down!

The catalog literally contained everything from A – Z; from accordions and ant farms to zip-up sweaters and zebra-print bedspreads. Each item was not only expertly photographed and carefully placed on the pages, but each also had well-written copy that enticed consumers of all ages. I could almost imagine Don Draper (John Hamm's character in *Mad Men*) hovering over a bottle of Brut or English Leather cologne, writing the line, "The distinctive scent that's always civilized, but never quite tame."

Before I got to the toys, I browsed through a 1960s fashion show. When's the last time you thought of turtlenecks with cardigans or Nehru jackets? Yet, there they were, in living color in the Sears Wishbook.

The prices were equally entertaining. Many were what you'd expect, given the value of the dollar in 1968. A package of two, D-cell batteries was 38 cents, and a ceramic ashtray with your family coat-of-arms sold for $2.79.

Other prices were unexpectedly high. Since the median household income in 1968 was less than $9,000, how difficult it must have been to afford a 23-inch color TV for $629.95, or an electric typewriter for $237.95.

Turning to page 168, the beginning of the toy section, was like opening the door to Santa's Workshop. It brought back a flood of memories—ghosts of Christmas toys past. Toys and games like Lincoln Logs ($3.88), Operation ($3.99), Time Bomb ($3.19), Rock 'em Sock 'em Robots ($9.99), the Hot Wheels Double-Dare Drag Set ($6.88), and Spirograph ($2.93) all made it from the pages of the Wishbook to a spot under our family's Christmas tree at one time or another, and there they were, as if frozen in time in the Sears Wishbook.

But the page that I stared at the longest was page 505 where I saw the GI Joe space capsule and suit. I was a boy of the '60s, so my toy box contained all things macho—Tonka trucks, Matchbox cars, and of course, GI Joe. GI Joe and all his accessories (what boy didn't have Joe's foot locker?) often led to conflicts on Thanksgiving morning as my brother and I were making our Christmas lists. The problems began if we both saw the same toy, in the catalog, at the same time. The disagreement was generally settled in one of two ways—either I'd put my brother in a headlock until he said "uncle," or my father would yell from behind his newspaper, "If you two don't knock it off, you'll get a couple Barbies instead of GI Joes."

As I thumbed through the pages of the 1968 Sears Wishbook, smiling and reminiscing, I realized that I wasn't just looking at an old catalog. Instead, it was like looking at a family album or a high school yearbook. The pages didn't hold merchandise, they held memories. The Wishbook was a 605 page time capsule, and I was lucky enough to be the one who opened it.

•

An Earth Day Lesson
(April 16, 2014)

Next week, we celebrate the 45th Earth Day.

April 22, 1970 was the first-ever event, when a very small group of people had the foresight to begin a consciousness-raising effort about the environment.

Some called that first occasion E-Day. But depending on the source, people weren't sure if the "E" stood for Environment Day or Earth Day. Regardless, now, all these years later, the movement that had such humble beginnings, has allowed baby boomers like me to breathe relatively clean air, to swim in fairly clean lakes, and enjoy reasonably verdant forests.

Environmentalists have had their detractors over the years, earning derogatory nicknames like "Nature-Boy" or "Tree Hugger." In fact, the first organizers of Earth Day were perceived as '60s hippies who channeled their anti-war protests into the pro-environment cause. No matter how they were regarded in the beginning, one has to wonder what our world would be like today without their efforts.

I've always said that I benefitted both academically and socially from a memorable group of teachers at St. Paul's Academy where I attended elementary school from kindergarten through eighth grade. Whether it was progressive-thinking nuns like Sister Ann Collins and Sister Elizabeth Snyder, or young educators like Dave Neal, John Vella, and Mike Caldwell, they guided a bunch of junior high schoolers through the often-confusing and turbulent late '60s and into the early 1970s.

My teachers are the reason I have a great Earth Day memory. I'm not sure if it was the first Earth Day in 1970, or the second one a year later, but I'm positive that the seventh and eighth graders at St. Paul's jumped on the Earth Day bandwagon. Why I recall this, I don't know, because there are no newspaper articles or old photos that document our participation. In fact, there's no mention of it either in our modest, mimeographed St. Paul's Academy yearbook or student newspaper *The SPA News & Views*. I can only attribute my memory of this Earth Day to that group of teachers who convinced a bunch of 12 and 13 year olds to protect and preserve the environment because it was going to be "our world" to live in.

What did we do to get involved with Earth Day? We walked, en masse, the two blocks from St. Paul's to East Park and planted a tree. It seems like a simple enough gesture, and far from earth-changing, but it remains etched in my memory. Curiosity got the best of me as I began writing about Earth Day, so I walked through East Park the other day, trying to figure out which tree "belonged to" the St. Paul's kids of 1970 and '71. I am certainly no trained arborist, so to me, one barren tree looked pretty much like the next. I needed some help, so I tracked down the city DPW tree supervisor, Jeff Hammill for assistance.

Jeff, who was probably just a toddler when the first Earth Day was celebrated, helped me narrow it down. I shared my story, and told him that I recall standing with my classmates facing East Fourth Street as we lowered a tree into a pre-dug hole. Jeff said that he has always wondered about a lone Ginkgo tree that is located along Fourth Street, among many trees more typical and native to our area. Though it's a very slow-growing tree, Jeff estimated that this Ginkgo is approximately 40 years old—an age that fits my timeline precisely.

Of course, the exact location or type of tree that we planted way-back-when doesn't really matter; what does matter is what that tree represents. On that short field trip to East Park one April day, a bunch of junior high kids learned an important life lesson. I think many people my age have become more environmentally conscious than previous generations. We have become the "green generation" that is known for conserving and recycling. We no longer drive big gas-guzzling cars and rarely do you see litter being thrown from car windows like people did habitually in the 1960s.

So we've come a long way. Now that we baby boomers are growing older, instead of it being "our earth" to care for like our former teachers cautioned, we're preserving it for our children and grandchildren—possibly because of a single tree planted in East Park forty-something years ago on one of the first Earth Days.

•

Not the Usual 'Treat'
(November 28, 2012)

We all have our favorite Halloween memories, many of which were captured in photographs. Some were possibly taken on a Polaroid in the 1970s, others with an iPhone last October.

The Halloween memory that came rushing back to me recently was courtesy of a resident of Building C at Sylvan Glen Apartments from the 1960s named Morgan.

First, some background. My parents were the property managers of Sylvan Glen, the forty-two unit complex at the corner of West Eighth and Van Buren Streets for the better part of twenty years in the 1960s and '70s.

Back then, the residents of Sylvan Glen seemed like a large, extended family. One-year leases turned into multi-year living arrangements because of the friendly atmosphere in the complex. Neighbors hung out on the cement steps of the buildings on hot summer nights, then helped dig each other's cars out of snow banks during epic Oswego blizzards.

Sylvan Glen in the 1960s was a gated community without a gate. Holidays were great because instead of single-family celebrations, many occasions included all tenants and their families. From July 4th picnics to Christmas parties, Sylvan Glen provided the setting of my wonder years.

Of all the holiday memories, the Halloween recollection that came rushing back to me recently was as vivid as if it happened yesterday. When trick-or-treaters rang the doorbell in apartment C-2, one of the basement apartments in building C, they got a *real* treat. (Remember the really cool-sounding two-tone door bells at Sylvan Glen?) When we rang that bell, we didn't get the usual candy bar, quarter, or even an apple. Instead, we got our pictures taken by our neighbor, Morgan, whose hobby was photography.

I understand that by today's standards, a mere photograph seems insignificant because just about everyone carries a camera phone at all times, and pictures get posted instantaneously for all the world to see on Facebook. But to an 11-year-old in 1968, getting a picture taken in full Halloween regalia was pretty

This 8 x 10 glossy photo was my Halloween treat in 1968.

neat. The deal was that a few days after Halloween, kids could return to the apartment and get an 8 x 10 black and white glossy of themselves for free! These pictures proved to be better than an apple, healthier than another candy bar, and more memorable than a 25-cent coin.

Over the years, these annual Halloween photos became cherished keepsakes for dozens of kids from the first ward, filling family albums and picture frames. At least a couple of these photos survived 40-plus years in my possession, and finding that photo recently brought back a flood of memories.

In addition to finding the photo of me as an 11-year-old werewolf in a bed sheet, I found one of my mom. As I mentioned, she was the property manager at Sylvan Glen, so by virtue of collecting rent checks and leasing the apartments, she knew all of the tenants. But on Halloween each year, as a thirty-something year-old mother of two, her goal was to go door-to-door in each of the seven buildings on Halloween, without being recognized. Most years she pulled it off! With her close friend Barbara Moody, they were disguised as everything from sorority girls to firefighters on various Halloween outings—and I have the pictures to prove it.

Now, on Halloween nights as I hand out Skittles and Kit-Kats, I can't help but think of Morgan, the photo keepsakes, and the special memories I have of Halloweens in Oswego thanks to him.

●

Everyone Old Enough Recalls 11/22/63
(November 13, 2013)

National political personality Bill O'Reilly has been on the *New York Times* best seller list for over a year with his book *Killing Kennedy*.

I'm never going to make the *New York Times* best seller list, but let's call this column *Saving Kennedy*.

Over the next ten days, the media will be leading up to the 50th anniversary of the assassination of President John F. Kennedy. There will be TV specials interviewing witnesses and survivors, computer-generated simulations of the shots that hit the motorcade, and talk show banter about conspiracy theories and what life in America would've been like had JFK served two full terms as president.

Simple math tells us that the sixty-year-olds of 2013 were the ten-year-olds of 1963. Anyone 60-plus can likely answer the question, "Where were you when you heard the news?" I'm just a little younger than that, so I don't remember hearing the news itself, but there are a lot of things I do remember.

I'm not sure how much my first grade teacher, Mrs. Gertrude English, knew about the shooting when the bell rang to end the school week on that Friday afternoon, but when I arrived home, despite being so young, I knew that something was terribly wrong. I don't recall ever seeing my mother, my great Aunt Helen or my grandmother cry before, but they were gathered around a flickering black and white TV with tears in their eyes.

Even after they explained it to me, I'm sure I didn't comprehend the magnitude of the tragedy. But to help occupy me during what was a very long weekend, my mom suggested I keep a scrapbook of all the newspaper articles. From a parenting standpoint, I now realize that it was probably a way for mom to cope with her grief while teaching her six-year-old a little about life and death. So mom, armed with her sewing shears and me with my rounded safety scissors, sat at the dining room table each day and cut out dozens of pictures from the *Palladium-Times*, *Post-Standard*, and the now-defunct *Herald-Journal*.

We took these clippings and crudely taped them on lined loose-leaf paper with scotch tape. Our three-ring binder paled in comparison to today's crafters' scrapbooks that are works of art. I have a good memory, but I remember these details, because as I'm writing this column, about 30 of these pages sit on my desk. Through almost five decades, a half-dozen moves, years of schooling, marriage, parenting, and teaching— basically through my entire lifetime—I have saved these mementos.

The tape has long-since lost its adhesiveness and the pages are a dingy yellow. But among the faded pages are photos of the Kennedys in the limo, Jackie in her blood-stained dress, and the touching salute from three-year-old John-John at the funeral. On the back of one such clipping from the Sunday *Herald-American* was an advertisement from P & C Markets stating, "All P & C stores will be closed on Monday, November 25 from 11:00 a.m. 'til 2:00 p.m. in due respect of President John Fitzgerald Kennedy."

Most of these images will be seen in retrospectives over the next two weeks or are easily available via an Internet search nowadays, but something has compelled me to hang on to this pile of brittle, faded, musty-smelling newspaper clippings all these years.

The most vivid image I have of that weekend fifty years ago, though, wasn't from TV or a newspaper, but from St. Paul's Church.

Since JFK was killed on a Friday, church on Sunday took on a different air. I distinctly remember a flag-draped casket in the middle aisle as we went to Sunday mass in the old St. Paul's Church on East Fifth and Mohawk. Unlike the grainy, black and white images on TV later that day as the body lay in state in the Capitol rotunda, the red, white, and blue flag covering a casket, right in our own church, brought the tragedy close to home.

History tells us that the president was buried on Monday, November 25, just three days before Thanksgiving of 1963. I really don't remember either of those days, but I can't imagine Americans having too much to be thankful for in the wake of the tragic killing of its young leader.

I've always been curious about the Kennedy era. Too young to comprehend it as a child, I've satisfied my curiosity several times as an adult. I've visited JFK's grave in Arlington National Cemetery on several occasions, and it seems to have a greater impact each time. Last November, my wife and I visited Dallas and went on a tour they call the "Kennedy Assassination Trail." From Love Field, through the parade route to Dealey Plaza—including the sixth floor museum in the Texas School Book Depository, we traced the locations of November 22, 1963. It was both fascinating (seeing Oswald's vantage point from the building) and eerie (an X marks the spot in the road where the first bullet hit JFK).

It's hard to believe, but next Friday marks the 50th anniversary of the day that the brief, shining moment, the Kennedy era known as Camelot, came to an end.

•

The Teacher Didn't Have Any Answers
(September 4, 2014)

The back-to-school sneakers have been tied, the backpacks are full, and the school buildings have been prepared, as teachers, lunch ladies, custodians, administrators, bus drivers, and of course, students head back to school today. I did that for all but six years of my life—on one side of the desk or the other—either as a student or a teacher.

During each of my 33 years as an educator, prior to retiring a year ago, the back-to-school excitement lasted well past Columbus Day, before settling into a nice, day-to-day routine.

Teachers pride themselves on trying to have all the answers for inquisitive students. Let's face it, if a student has a question, whether it's a first grader wondering why the sky is blue or a high school senior inquiring about a calculus equation, it's not good to reply "I don't know." A teacher is supposed to be the "sage on the stage." A teacher is supposed to know the answers. A teacher is supposed to be prepared.

That's why I always reflect, at this time of the year, on a day I didn't have *any* answers—September 11, 2001.

The back-to-school excitement was everywhere. The freshly waxed floors from summer custodial work still had a beautiful shine. The new school clothes hadn't all been worn yet. After all, it was only the first Tuesday of the 2001-02 academic year, and the fifth day of school overall—a gorgeous early September day. It was the kind of day that, if it wasn't so early in the year, someone might consider playing hooky.

What soon transpired was the first historical "day of infamy" that I had to face in my adult life. Of the other two "where-were-you-when-you-heard-the-news" historical moments, one happened before I was born (Pearl Harbor, December 7, 1941) and the other, when I was in first grade (President Kennedy's assassination on November 22, 1963.)

I know all too well that some Oswegonians view educators negatively, but I don't think any of the naysayers would've wanted to trade places with a teacher on 9/11. Why? Think back on that day twelve years ago. When *you* saw the horror, from the initial impact of the planes, to the jumpers from high above the New York City skyline, to the collapse of the towers and the ensuing rescue efforts; what did *you* do? Maybe you worked somewhere where you could get comfort from co-workers. Maybe you were self-employed, so you could take a walk, look skyward, and wonder. Maybe you were able to go an Oswego church that opened its doors on that Tuesday morning.

But teachers were left to do their jobs, to be role models of composure, caring, and compassion in front of classes of curious students of all ages. They had to try to keep their own emotions in check, though difficult to do as some colleagues wept during free time and wondered if their friends or family members who lived in New York City were safe.

Ernest Hemingway once said that "guts" is grace under pressure. I was proud of my teaching colleagues that day. They showed a lot of guts.

I remember distinctly being in a study hall, with about thirty juniors and sophomores watching the tragedy unfold on television just as the first tower crumbled. Scott Merry, who coincidentally is now a teacher himself, was an eleventh grader sitting in the front seat. He watched, and then simply asked, "Mr. McCrobie, what's going on?" Obviously, Scott was a high school junior, so he didn't need me to explain the fact that someone had flown a plane into a building and it had subsequently fallen down. That's not what he was asking. From the look on his face and the incredulous tone of his voice, I knew what his question meant. He needed to know what was going on with our world.

And I didn't have the answer.

There were, of course, lots of other good questions posed to a helpless teacher who had his own inquiries. As kids started being picked up by their parents, the ones who remained asked why everyone was going home.

I didn't have the answer.

Others wondered if the nuclear plants, right in our backyard, would be targeted by terrorists.

I didn't have the answer.

Some asked out loud, "What kind of person would crash a plane into a building full of innocent people?"

I definitely didn't have the answer to that one.

I did have the answer to one question that day. One of my journalism students (high school journalists, like their professional counterparts, are usually inquisitive) asked if "things" would ever be the same.

Unfortunately, I knew the answer to that one was "no."

It's been more than a decade since 9/11/01, and I'd love to say that I've come up with all the answers that escaped me on that day of infamy at Oswego High School. But I haven't; I'm not sure anyone has.

•

A Fair Day? No, A Great Day!
(August 20, 2014)

The New York State Fair opens tomorrow, and though it's a quick trip up Route 690 from Oswego, it's not a trip my family ever made when I was a kid. But I have a great memory of the State Fair nonetheless.

My first trip to the Fair was in the early '70s when I was about 14. I went with a bunch of my buddies and I'm pretty sure we were like the packs of teenagers who roam the Fair or Harborfest nowadays. We were loud, rambunctious, and annoying to everyone over the age of 50. The only difference is that we didn't have cell phones.

One August day, bored with our summer routine, we somehow got the idea to go to the Fair. Too young to drive ourselves and too cool to be seen in somebody's mom's station wagon, we decided to take the bus. The bus would take us from the S & O bus station on West Second Street directly to the front gate of the Fair. Our parents knew we were going, so it's not like we ran away from home to join the circus.

Needless to say, we were excited. For most of us, it was our first trip to the Fair. The prospect of an all-day trip with no adult supervision was pretty cool. Two things stick out in my memory about the bus ride. First, it took too long. We were anxious to get there, so the annoying stops to pick up more fairgoers in Fulton and Phoenix were like speed bumps delaying our journey. The second thing that I recall about the bus trip was the advice I got about the return ride home. I distinctly remember my father telling me that the last bus was scheduled to leave the Fairgrounds at 11:00 p.m. Dad's advice was more of a warning than just a fatherly suggestion: "Don't miss it, because I'm not driving to Syracuse at that hour to pick you guys up!" (I'm positive he meant what he said.)

When we arrived at the Fair, we were on a sensory overload—the sights, the sounds, the smells that immediately overwhelmed us were nothing like we had experienced at the little traveling carnivals that came to Oswego on the July 4th weekend every summer.

Then and now, midway barkers love to see groups of teenage boys heading their way without parents or chaperones. With cash in our pockets, we were fresh meat for the sharks of the carnival. We fell for every challenge we saw. Toss a ring onto the rim of a Coke bottle? Sure. Shoot on oversized basketball into an undersized hoop? Why not. Ring a bell with the strong-man's sledge hammer? We'll give it a try. Knock down a pyramid of weighted metal milk bottles with a baseball? Piece of cake.

That was all good fun, but there was little risk involved in those games. We came to the Fair for excitement and adventure, so we headed for the rides, the Freak Show, and the Burlesque Show.

The closest thing to a thrill ride for me up to that point in my life was riding to Fair Haven with my grandmother driving. Gram was an aggressive driver with a full-blooded Irishman's temper and the vocabulary of a truck driver. But on this trip to the Fair, I was going to face my fears of heights and spinning rides both at the same time. The ride was called the Skydiver. It was appropriately named, but at least real skydivers have parachutes. The Skydiver is a ride with cars mounted on a circular frame like a Ferris wheel, but the cars also spin on a front-back axis similar to a barrel roll. It didn't take me long on the Skydiver to realize that my lunch combination of cotton candy, chocolate milk and onion rings had been a bad idea. Though I was able to avoid losing my lunch, I did lose lots of coins that rattled around in this contraption while we were spinning and rolling high above Solvay.

With feet firmly planted on the ground again, our gang was lured into the Freak Show. Though curiosities such as The Man with Three Eyes and the World's Smallest Pony left me with a memory, it wasn't a recollection of how impressed I was; it was the remembrance of being duped into plunking down good money to see these scams.

Finally, it was time for the boys to become men. We headed towards the Burlesque Show. "Girls! Girls! Girls!" the guy out front barked. "Gentlemen only." We figured though most of us were only 14 or 15, we could still talk our way in. What we didn't take into consideration was that we looked more like we were 12 than 18. Needless to say, we were turned away before we could even get the money out of our wallets.

We did lots of other things that day, but after the sun set, we were sure to heed my dad's warning, and catch the last bus home.

I've had some enjoyable days at the Fair since that first trip, but the feelings of camaraderie and independence that we enjoyed that day so long ago come flooding back each year when the Fair rolls around.

•

Mike McCrobie

3

PORT CITY PEOPLE

Mike McCrobie

Santa Lived on East Seneca Street

(December 25, 2013)

According to the Bible, Mary's husband, St. Joseph, was a carpenter. So it's somewhat coincidental that to a generation of Oswego kids, Santa Claus was also a carpenter.

Every December, for fifteen years, Gary Baker, a union carpenter by day, became Santa Claus at night, and his East Seneca Street home became the North Pole.

If you talk to Gary, like I did recently, it's easy to understand how important family is to him and his wife Linda. That's why, what started as a simple Christmas light display for their young son Ryan in 1982, turned into an Oswego holiday tradition. It wasn't uncommon for up to 500 kids per night to visit the Baker house and wave to Santa, enjoy the lights, get a piece of candy, or drop a letter in Santa's mailbox out front.

People didn't have GPS back in those days, but the lights served as a beacon, directing minivans full of families to the Bakers' home. Others may have been guided by the Christmas music or traced the line of kids from the corner of East Ninth and Seneca Streets back to the Baker property.

But to call what the Bakers did a "light display" would be like calling Yankee Stadium just another ballpark. At its peak, 18,000 lights adorned the 99 East Seneca Street property, decorating everything from the garage to the family swimming pool out back. Lighted arches traversed the driveway and toy soldiers stood sentry over the visitors. Though the Bakers never took a penny from anyone to offset their costs, they welcomed some help on what Gary called two "prized possessions" in the display. Former Kingsford Park teacher, master craftsman, and long-time friend of the Bakers, Chris Zollo and some of his art students constructed a church that was a big part of the Bakers' holiday display. And Gary's mother created a nativity scene from scratch, with costume jewelry that she gathered at local garage sales.

A cornerstone of the Bakers' display was a mailbox for letters to Santa. (I distinctly remember a cold December night when a young father of four, braved sub-freezing temperatures to place four letters in that very mailbox. I recall that so vividly, because that young dad was me!) Linda Baker (let's call her Mrs. Claus) read every letter that was placed in the box, according to Gary, and occasionally replied to some of the more heartfelt requests.

How much work did it take to assemble such an extravaganza? "I never looked at it as work," Gary said when we reminisced. "I'd work a 10-hour day on construction, but it never bothered me to come home and play Santa Claus." The lights and figurines came out of storage just after Halloween and the Bakers would have a family get-together every December 1 to turn on the display for the season. The schedule for the Bakers was simple. The lights were on and Santa was outside every night from 6:00 – 9:00 p.m. until December 23 (Santa had to begin his worldwide travels on Christmas Eve). This was a nightly labor of love in both good weather and bad, and with their second-ward home located just a few blocks from the lake, there were plenty of nights when the winds howled through Santa-Gary's red suit.

But it wasn't just Oswego kids who drove over the river and through the woods to see the Bakers' house. People came from all over. Gary recalled families regularly coming in from Fulton and Mexico, and even a group from Canada visiting.

Gary's inspiration for his family's display came from growing up in the city he loves—Oswego. "As a kid, my dad would drive us around to see the lights, and I always remembered the Sweetings' house on the corner of Ontario and Bronson," he recalled. His childhood memories of Oswego in the 1960s and his observations of Oswego in the '80s, fueled his passion to give people a holiday display to enjoy. "Fewer and fewer people were decorating in the early '80s, so I wanted to go all out," he stated.

What's December like now for a "retired" Santa Claus? There are new holiday traditions for Gary Baker. He has a grandson, he takes his family to Lights on the Lake in Syracuse, and enjoys something he, ironically, never had time for in those "Santa years"—Christmas shopping. But he cautioned me not to say "retired Santa." In fact, the Bakers are back up to about 8,000 lights decorating their home, and he's even purchased a new Santa suit, though he admits, for now, it's not for hundreds of kids like back in the day. Instead, it's just for one very special little boy—his grandson.

•

Local Barbers Were a Cut Above
(February 5, 2014)

Oswego of the 1960s was a hometown where it seemed like everyone knew one another. Sometimes, you might have only known someone by their first name and occupation such as "Pete the Bookie," "Jimmy the Tailor," or "Dan the Mailman."
But there was something folksy about that.

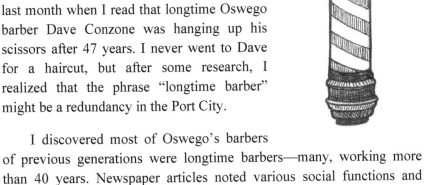

In the same vein that Andy Griffith's Mayberry had Floyd the Barber, Oswego had "_____ the Barber" (you fill in the blank with any one of a couple dozen names.)

I began thinking about Oswego's barbers last month when I read that longtime Oswego barber Dave Conzone was hanging up his scissors after 47 years. I never went to Dave for a haircut, but after some research, I realized that the phrase "longtime barber" might be a redundancy in the Port City.

I discovered most of Oswego's barbers of previous generations were longtime barbers—many, working more than 40 years. Newspaper articles noted various social functions and testimonial dinners where members of Oswego Barbers' Local #303 gathered to honor their own. Thomas "Irish" Connelly (55 years), Joseph Crisafulli (55 years), Alfred D'Amico (62 years), Jimmy Scandura (50 years), Joseph Occhino (43 years) all showed amazing longevity for men who spent their entire working days on their feet.

A 1961 *Palladium-Times* article, identified 26 members of Oswego Barbers union #303. Among them were Vic Cafalone, Harry Melita, and Domenic and Anthony Cortese. Listed in the 1973 city directory were names more familiar to me such as Dina Scandura, Bill Hoefer, Dominic Pezzlo, John Sanford, and Sam Cutro.

What struck me as I read more about the barbers of yesteryear was that, like so many men of "the greatest generation," they took such pride in their craft. While their contemporaries toiled in area factories producing matches at the Diamond Match, chocolate at Long's Candy Works, or boilers at Cyclotherm, these craftsmen took pride in the appearance of all Oswego men.

The barber-customer relationship is one of both familiarity and loyalty. I have had a handful of dentists, many doctors, and dozens of teachers in my lifetime, but I have only had three barbers. I started with Sammy Cutro, because, like so many businesses of the early 1960s, Sammy was the neighborhood barber. Whether I was pushed in a stroller as an infant or walked with my grandpa as a toddler, we'd trek the three blocks down East Seneca Street from the house to Sammy's shop at East 10th and Seneca. I'm not sure how many years he cut my hair, but I know it was long enough for me to graduate from the booster seat into the full-sized barber chair. The haircut would end with a sucker, and to this day I recall trying to figure out how to get freshly cut hair off of a sticky sucker!

In the late '60s the hair styles of men and boys were lengthening—everywhere except in my house. My father's pet peeve was long hair. Every time he'd see a teenage boy with long hair, he would either mumble the word "hippie," or say, "He looks like a girl." If I wanted to test my father's powers of observation, I'd let the hair hit the top of my ears. That was his benchmark, his measuring stick. If my hair was touching my ears at all, he'd say one simple phrase, "You're looking a little shabby." I knew that "shabby" meant get to Irish Connelly's barber shop.

Irish was the second of my trio of barbers. He was a close friend of my dad, so he knew what would be expected when I got home. As a pre-teen, I'd look longingly at the pictures on the wall of Irish's West First Street establishment that showed cool haircuts like "the shag," much longer and more stylized than the cut I was getting.

Once, when I was about thirteen, I tested the limits and asked Irish for "just a trim." We both knew it wouldn't go over well when I got home, but he honored my wishes. Needless to say, that night's dinner conversation went something like this . . .

DAD: "Wasn't the barbershop open today?"

ME: "Yeah. I got my haircut."

DAD: "Go back tomorrow and get another one."

End of conversation.

Irish passed away in the 1970s and when he closed up shop, I began going to Becky Henderson at Dominic's. She moved around to various salons over the years before purchasing the Oak Hill Barbershop from Jimmy Scandura. She'll kill me for saying this, but Becky has cut my hair for about 40 years. She has cut it when it was long and short, when it was jet black and now salt-n-pepper. She has cut my hair before many of my life's milestones, from graduations to job interviews; weddings to funerals. And as I stood by, with camera-in-hand, Becky snipped away the baby-fine hair of my four children, giving them their first haircuts.

Times have changed and the old smoke-filled barbershops where men gathered to talk sports and politics have given way to stylists and salons, but the relationships and the memories of the old union shops linger like the scent of talcum powder on a freshly shaven neck.

•

A Cup of Coffee with a Childhood Idol
(February 6, 2013)

You wouldn't know it by looking outside, but spring is here. Not meteorological spring, but baseball spring.

Next week, pitchers and catchers will report to places like Lakeland, Florida and Scottsdale, Arizona to begin the preseason ritual known as spring training. But for the first time in 25 years, Jon Matlack won't be heading South.

You remember Jon Matlack. Mets fans, like me, certainly do. Jon Matlack, struck out over 1,500 major league batters. He was the 1972 National League Rookie of the Year and co-MVP of the 1975 All-Star game. His career ERA is lower than half of the pitchers in the Hall of Fame. He threw a masterful two-hit shutout against the Big Red Machine of Cincinnati in the 1973 National League Championship series. His locker was sandwiched between Tom Seaver's and Jerry Koosman's in the Mets' clubhouse. And Jon Matlack now lives here in Oswego.

As a kid of the '70s, summers in my neighborhood were filled with pick-up baseball games. We didn't create players on an *MLB 2K 13* video game; we mimicked our favorite major league stars on the sandlot. Whether it was Rod Carew's batting stance, Pete Rose's headfirst slides, or Jon Matlack's signature leg kick, we loved to imitate our heroes.

That's why it was a thrill for me—even as a retired 55-year-old—to sit down, and talk baseball over a cup of coffee last week with one of my baseball heroes, Jon Matlack.

Jon lives in Oswego part of the year, and after a 13 year major league playing career that ended in 1983, has been back in the game for the past 25 years as a minor league pitching coordinator for several organizations, most recently the Houston Astros.

Jon's easy to talk to. He loves the game of baseball and didn't mind spending a morning last week answering questions about all things

baseball, from philosophical changes in the game to last Wednesday's
sport page headline about
performance enhancing drugs.

Matlack grew up in West
Chester, PA, and if the Mets
hadn't used their first round draft
choice on him in 1967, he likely
would have accepted an
appointment to the U.S. Military
Academy at West Point. Just as I
idolized Mets pitchers of the early
'70s, he admired another pretty
good left-hander who wore
number 32, Sandy Koufax. He
met Koufax years later at a charity
golf event, and was amazed at the
size of the Hall-of-Famer's hands,
which I couldn't imagine being much larger than Matlack's, whose right
hand swallowed mine when we shook hands, as if he was throwing a
four-seam fastball.

Clearly, Jon Matlack is a communicator, which served him well as
an instructor in the Padres, Tigers, White Sox, and Astros organizations.
He talks of goals, high expectations, and focus. Like most teachers, he
enjoys his interaction with young players. "It's easier to
obtain their trust. They listen," he said.

Though decades removed from his playing days, one can see why a
kid from rural Pennsylvania made it to the big time. "All my friends just
assumed we were going to be pro athletes. I'm a hard-headed Dutchman.
Stubborn. It was a forgone conclusion that we would do whatever it took
to get there," he said.

Now 63 and a grandfather of seven, Jon is appreciative of the
positive influences he had along the way. He is quick to give credit
where credit is due to everyone from Charlie Perrone, his high school
coach, to Mets' teammates "Tommy and Koos" (Seaver and Koosman)

and Hall of Famer Willie Mays.

Being a baseball "lifer," Matlack is concerned about the future of the game and what he called specialization. Moneyball is a popular trend in baseball with statistical analyses done by computers instead of baseball men with instincts. He's not a fan of guys who never played the game making those kinds of decisions. "The game has changed to the point where the computer is predicting probability. It's like taking a fantasy baseball team and putting it out on the field. It takes the human element away and team chemistry disappears."

Of course, no discussion of New York baseball is complete without at least one Yogi Berra story. Matlack, who recently saw the 88-year-old legend at the Baseball Assistance Team (B.A.T.) fundraising dinner in New York, said that Seaver gave him the best advice about dealing with then-manager Berra. Matlack confided he often couldn't understand Berra when he came to the mound, so he asked the more experienced Seaver what he should do. The Mets ace told Matlack, "If Yogi comes out with his hand out, hand him the ball and jog off the field. If his hand isn't out, just say 'OK' when he's done talking, and *he'll* run back to the dugout!"

But it's a bittersweet time for Jon Matlack. For over forty springs, as a player or a coach, he's packed his bags every February and headed to spring training. But the Astros are going in a different direction with their young pitchers, so Jon is out of work.

It's too bad, because baseball, in its current state, could use a few good men like Jon Matlack.

•

More Than Just Our Weatherman
(January 8, 2014)

The anatomy of a snow day in the 1960s for most Oswego kids began by tuning into radio station WSGO, 1440 on the AM dial, about 6:45 a.m. to listen to the weather forecast. From there, the school closing announcements would often come, breakfast would hurriedly be eaten, gray woolen socks and boots would be pulled on over snow pants, and out the door we'd go.

Somehow, in the minds and memories of Oswego kids, this sequence of events, and so many snow day recollections, began with the gravelly-voice of meteorologist Bob Sykes on the radio.

Long before there was a national cable TV weather channel or an entire "storm team" on local television, a generation of Oswegonians grew up with "our weatherman," Bob Sykes. Calling him our weatherman was not merely his job title, but a term of endearment.

In the decades in which Bob dispersed weather information, technology was limited. There was no Internet or text message alert system and if Sykes saw swirls of purple, green, and yellow, they weren't on a Doppler radar screen, but on the tie-dye t-shirts that his college students wore. Back then, weather predictions were often based on the experience and passion of the forecaster, and no one had more experience or passion than Bob Sykes.

I was lucky enough recently to get some transcripts of Bob's own notes from his son, Robert (who may be remembered by his Oswego friends as Bruce), a prominent attorney in Utah. To Bob, the weather was not just his vocation, but his avocation. As a respected, high-profile educator, Bob turned down personal opportunities because of his passion for weather. He was asked to chair the Earth Science Department at SUNY Oswego and he was approached to run for the Oswego City School District Board of Education, but declined both opportunities. In his own words, Bob explained his reasons, while professing his infatuation with Oswego's weather. "I did not believe I could give the effort and devotion that I thought the jobs required because of my overwhelming interests in lake weather studies, especially during the winter," Sykes professed.

Rick Gessner, son of former WSGO owner Bob Gessner, has lots of memories of Sykes. One of his favorite stories, grew out of Sykes' zeal for talking about the weather and occasional conflicts this caused with

FCC guidelines. "It was hard for Bob to adhere to the strict time requirements that went along with radio station programming," Gessner said. "Programs were timed to the second and WSGO's news programming started as soon as the sweep-second hand arrived at the top of each hour. Our staff asked Bob if he could end his weather forecast promptly before the top of the hour. Bob quite often had trouble wrapping up his forecast to coincide with the start of the news segments, so a staff member came up with the 'Bob Sykes bye-bye tape.' This was an eight second tape that was taken from a previously recorded segment that Bob had done, at the end of which he would say, 'This is Bob Sykes, chief meteorologist for the State University of New York at Oswego, reporting for WSGO.' When it appeared that Bob would 'run overtime' into the news segment, the on-duty engineer at the radio station would slap in the 'Bob Sykes bye-bye tape,' at exactly eight seconds before the top of the hour, and the news segment started right on time!"

Oswego resident Al Moreau grew up in the Town of Oswego neighborhood where the Sykes family resided. As a child, Moreau recalls seeing the distinguished college professor lying on his back in the middle of Brown Drive, looking skyward, to analyze wind direction and bands of snow.

Countless SUNY Oswego students, whether undergrads fulfilling an elective, or meteorology majors preparing for a career, were led to the rooftop of Piez Hall, in good weather and bad, to experience the weather first-hand from professor Sykes.

Bob's excitement for the weather was never more evident than during the infamous Blizzard of '66. His personal notes estimated that during that five-day period in January, he broadcast on the radio some 150 times.

As kids listening to "the information station" WSGO, we didn't realize what a true expert professor Sykes was. Heck, we were just kids hanging our hopes for a snow day on his forecasts. But Sykes was a true pioneer in the field of meteorology, with an obvious specialization in lake effect snow. In fact, Sykes is credited with coining the meteorological term "snowburst," and distinguishing this type of snow event from other similar weather terms such as "squall" and "blizzard."

In a November 1978 column that appeared in the *Palladium-Times*, writer Bob Whittemore quipped, "You can tell it's winter when 'Bob Sykes' becomes a household word around the city and county."

I recently read that current SUNY Oswego meteorology professor Scott Steiger received a $320,000 grant to study lake effect snow storms. The grant provides high-tech equipment to travel into the heart of lake effect snowstorms the way storm chasers pursue tornados in the Midwest.

Somewhere from the heavens, Bob Sykes is looking down on this next generation of meteorology study--and smiling.

•

The 'Old Guard' Tradition
(March 20, 2013)

The table is rectangular, not round. There is no sword in a stone, nor is there a wizard named Merlin. But I'm fortunate enough to attend a monthly gathering that, in my eyes, is every bit as legendary as King Arthur's Knights of the Round Table.

In a tradition that dates back to the 1950s, one Thursday evening each month, a group of retired Oswego teachers gathers at Vona's to socialize, reminisce, and pretend to solve all the world's problems over dinner.

One cannot look around the table without realizing the impact that these men have had on generations of Oswego students and our community.

By virtue of my retirement in June of 2012, I'm the new kid on the block, the novice, the rookie in the group. I was a little apprehensive when I sat down recently for my first such gathering, because for me, these men aren't just former colleagues, but some are my former teachers as well. These educators not only shaped the lives of *other* Oswego kids, but many of them had an immeasurable effect on my life as well.

I wasn't sure if I should raise my hand to ask my American history teacher's permission to use the restroom, or if I really should ask my old health teacher to pass me the salt knowing what he taught me years ago about high blood pressure!

A look around the table made me realize that there's hardly any aspect of our lives that these men haven't influenced. They taught Oswego everything from how to parallel park (John Steinfeld, Joe Rotolo) to the Pythagorean Theorem (Mike Caldwell, Jerry Pooler). They nurtured an appreciation of literature (Tom Frawley, Bill Runeari) and an understanding of government and law (Joe Sgarlata, Charlie Young). We learned photography and woodworking from Jan Noyes and Bill Bellow, who sit across from me. When OHS had a business department, Pete Bock and Lou Crisafulli gave kids fundamentals in accounting, office practice and keyboarding. At the end of the table, Bill Symons, whose instruction in physical education classes and on the athletic field made him a Hall of Fame coach, talks to health teacher Gary Carter, who passes along life lessons he learned while playing football at Penn State for Joe Paterno.

The conversations are what you might expect from a group of retired educators. Like an artist who, in the twilight of his career, can finally step back and admire a painting created years before, these men often reminisce about what some call their "success stories." A success story is a former student, now likely a middle-aged man or woman, who grew and flourished just like that seedling we all placed in the cup back in kindergarten. These men are the ones who cultivated those seeds, nurtured skills, developed talents, piqued interests, and now read or see or hear of former students' accomplishments with pride.

These mentors and role models talk about those who preceded them, the previous generation of Oswego educators who steered them towards the classroom and a teaching career. The names are mentioned with reverence and respect: Dave Powers, Anthony Slosek, Sylvester Goodrich, Fred Maxon, Muriel Cole, Walt Beck, Bob Richardson, Sister Mary Paul and countless others.

They talk of the teaching profession past, present and future. Driver Ed. teachers recall near misses with student drivers on the road and wood shop teachers chime in with near catastrophes with a bandsaw. Bob Zuber, Mike Lynn, and Rotolo discuss the passion for sailing they passed along to students via the Sailing Club. Coaches like Symons and Bill Fatiga relive the glory days of Buccaneer athletics and lament the decline of the three-sport athlete.

They bristle and just shake their heads at the mention of Columbine and Sandy Hook.

The origin of this assemblage goes back to the 1950s when legendary Oswego educators like Ralph Faust, Len Lambert, Phil Fleishman, Frank Reed, Elliot Smith, Ralph Konduct, and Mel McFee met to socialize outside of school. According to Symons, who does roll call for the monthly dinners now, stated, "They called themselves 'The Old Guard.' They always met on Thursdays and always at Vona's, so we've continued that custom."

Why carry on the tradition? To Symons, this fraternity of educators is simply a bunch of guys who worked together for 20, 30 or sometimes 40 years, who generally got along, and just want to stay connected.

Though Oswego is not Camelot, and these educators have neither vanquished the Saxons nor rescued damsels in distress like King Arthur's Knights, they have won many battles. In doing so, they helped make Oswego a better place through their teaching, guidance, and example. This group's Holy Grail was not a lost treasure, but a quest to improve our community by producing well-rounded and well-educated students, who would become good citizens.

●

4

OUR TOWN

Where Were You Every April 1?

(April 2, 2014)

We turned our calendars to April 1 yesterday.

To many, April Fool's Day is a day of harmless pranks, but to several generations of Oswegonians, April 1 was always a special day for another reason—the opening of Nunzi's.

Aging Port City baby boomers all remember Nunzi's. Whether we were "townies" in softball uniforms or SUNY Oswego students; construction workers building Nine Mile or just-turned-eighteen-year olds with their brand new sheriff's ID cards, Nunzi's was a place where memories were made.

For those under age 50, or anyone new to the area, a brief history lesson is in order. Nunzi's was located just off Snake Swamp Road (appropriately named because it literally wound through the swamp like a snake with its twists and turns. (Today, Snake Swamp Road is called Lakeshore Road; less ominous sounding I suppose.) One right turn off that road led patrons down a bumpy path to Nunzi's, literally sitting on the shore of Lake Ontario, just east of Camp Hollis. It almost appeared in the darkness out of nowhere, like a mirage to a desert traveler, lit up by the neon beer signs in the windows against the darkness of both the lake and nightfall.

Nunzi's would never make *Better Homes & Gardens* magazine for it décor, but its beauty was measured in other ways.

At least three generations sat on the tree stumps-turned-bar-stools at Nunzi's before it closed in the early 1990s.

What did we like about Nunzi's? What didn't we like! My friends Jerry Brown, Al Nessel, Sam Natoli, and I were always pretty tight with the dollar (in other words, we were teenage cheapskates). We were regulars at the Tuesday and Thursday night kill-a-keg promotion. Owner Sam Tesoriero would provide a free half-keg of Genesee Cream Ale until it was empty. The lucky drinker who got the last cup from the keg before it turned to foam would get a free case of Genny Cream cans handed to him/her right across the bar. Try as I might to time it just right, I was never the lucky winner of those coveted green cans.

Of course, hanging out with friends and meeting new ones made Nunzi's the place to be, but there were also other entertainment options. The foosball table, just inside the door to the left, was rarely idle, and often had several quarters lined on its ledge, ready for opponents to challenge the winners. Likewise with the pool table in the back, where players often had to ask bar patrons to move from the cramped space so they didn't have to alter their shots.

I was never very good at pool or foosball, but I loved to play the bowling machine along the west wall, near the restrooms. That aging arcade game would keep six of us entertained for hours, while satisfying our competitive spirits. Our unwritten rule was that the two low scorers would have to buy drinks for the two winners, while the middle two would get a "pass."

For other entertainment, you could head to the back porch and beyond onto the rocky beach, literally a stone's throw from Lake Ontario. Out back was just an extension of the bar itself. On any given night, people could witness a gorgeous Oswego sunset, a couple good boyfriend/girlfriend arguments, and an occasional skinny dip. There is no documentation of any "submarine races" ever held behind Nunzi's.

The soundtrack of Nunzi's was provided by its jukebox. I'm not certain how many records the old jukebox held, but to be honest, it really didn't matter. People only associate one song with Nunzi's, "Build Me Up Buttercup" by the Foundations. By the time I turned the drinking age (okay, I might have snuck in a few times before that), "Build Me Up Buttercup" was already an oldie, but it was the unofficial anthem of Nunzi's nonetheless. If patrons didn't hear it dozens of times a night, the jukebox was either broken or unplugged because someone had heard "Buttercup" fifteen consecutive times.

Nunzi's was crowded, noisy, and so much fun. In fact, my friend Gene Tracy used to refer to it as "Funzi's."

Nunzi's, in 1965, before the wooden doors were replaced with screens for the summer, according to Sam Tesoriero's daughter, Peg Wiltsie, who provided this photo from the family album. The neon signs in the windows display popular beers of the era: Carling Black Label, Schaefer, Genesee, and Utica Club.

We never felt bad if we spilled a beer because the wooden-plank floors were older than our grandparents. One friend of mine (who shall remain nameless just in case the statute of limitations hasn't expired), for some unknown reason, enjoyed punching holes in the ceiling when the urge came over him during a heated foosball match.

Nunzi's was technically called Nunzi's Lakeside Tavern, but it was so much more. To Oswegonians, it was a reward given to us every April 1, for having survived six months of winter. It was a welcome harbinger of spring and it buoyed our hopes for an endless summer.

•

Christmas Shopping Circa 1973
(November 27, 2013)

Saturday is the third annual Small Business Saturday, a day created by the American Express Company that is sandwiched between Black Friday and Cyber Monday to further remind us that the holiday shopping frenzy is upon us.

Black Friday is geared towards the giant big-box stores and Cyber Monday focuses on e-commerce (online shopping), but Small Business Saturday encourages Americans to shop locally. Of these three shopping fests, I like Small Business Saturday the most, not only because it spotlights the little guy, but because it allows me to reminisce about the days when just about *all* shopping was done locally at small businesses.

So, for old time's sake I'm not shopping in 2013. Instead, come along with me on a shopping trip in the Oswego of 1973. (Since I don't yet have a driver's license, we'll have to walk downtown.)

As I head south on West First Street, I see Stoney's Auto Parts on the corner of West First and Cayuga Streets. Although my dad loves to detail his brand new '74 model year Pontiac Bonneville, even he would be disappointed if I got him a tub of Turtle Wax for a Christmas gift, so I dismiss that idea and keep walking.

Since nobody can shop on an empty stomach, I have to stop at 154 West First Street at Matott's Bakery for a half-moon cookie. (I need to break the big $50 bill I got when I cashed my Oswego City Savings Bank Christmas Club check anyway.)

My next two stops will be at storefronts south of Matott's—Aero Sporting Goods and Fuddy's Ontario Sporting Goods. At Aero, I can pick up a model fire truck for my 13-year-old brother to assemble. At Fuddy's, I shop for myself. I need a new pair of blue and white "Oswego Phys. Ed." gym shorts and matching t-shirt, so my gym teacher, Mr. Symons, doesn't holler at me for not being dressed properly for PE.

Next to Fuddy's is Mr. Pidgeon's liquor store, but me buying a

Christmas gift there is out of the question. Though the drinking age is eighteen, a sixteen-year-old who doesn't yet shave and looks like he's twelve, has no chance to buy a bottle of holiday cheer.

My great Aunt Helen is a devout Catholic, so some type of religious pin or a rosary will be perfect for her. I can get her gift at one of the downtown jewelers (Dufore's, Raymond's, or Schneider's), at Ange's Gifts (173 West First), near "Irish" Connelly's barber shop, or at the Thunderbird, the eclectic gift shop on West Second Street.

The Thunderbird Gift Shop on West Second Street offered an interesting array of gifts for Oswego shoppers of bygone days.

There are plenty of options for women's clothing for mom in town. The iconic Shapiro's for women at the busy intersection of West First and Bridge (diagonal from Green's five-and-ten store) has all of the trendy '73 styles. Crossing Bridge Street, next to Marine Midland Bank is McDonald's, with a more sophisticated line of high-end women's fashions.

I guess if apparel is the answer for the men on my list, I probably could go to Sterio's Men's Shop or do one-stop-shopping in the two-story clothing store at 25 West Bridge—Kline's. I can pick up a flannel shirt for grandpa and a sweater for dad at Kline's, but if I can't find just the right thing there, I can head to the east side to Shapiro's Men's Shop or Frank G. Wells. I'm familiar with the salespeople at Wells' in the Midtown Center because that's where the chubby McCrobie boys have bought their "husky" pants for years!

If it's not clothing for dad (he always returns everything we get him anyway), I can head back west to CJ's Bookstore (corner of West Second and Bridge) for a paperback or maybe a 1974 desk calendar from E.S. Howard's a half block to the west.

I don't have a girlfriend to buy for, but all the cool high school and college kids shop for their bell bottoms and peasant blouses at either Barry's Outlet (9 West Bridge St.), The Stall (41 West Bridge St.), the Clothing Junction (West First and Bridge in the historic Buckhout Building) or at the Etc. Shop on Washington Blvd., on the way to SUCO. I like shopping at Barry's, but the proprietor, Mae Tompkins, watches high school kids suspiciously, like we're all reincarnations of Bonnie & Clyde about to rob the place.

Like Syracuse's "auto row" on West Genesee Street, Oswego has "shoe store row." Three choices—Endicott Johnson (199 West First St.), Vona's Shoes (203 West First St.), and Modern Shoe (202 West First St.). Modern Shoe also has the repair shop in the back to sew torn leather or put cool-sounding taps on the heels of penny loafers. These three businesses meet every Oswegonian's footwear needs from slippers to platform shoes; from earth shoes to Bates' Floaters.

A weary shopper traipsing through downtown Oswego circa 1973, can work up an appetite, so a stop for a bite to eat at Savas' will get me through the rest of the day.

"The Sidewalks of New York" song lyric says "East side, west side, all around the town," but it could be talking about the Oswego of 1973, not the Big Apple. I'm not alone downtown in '73. Everywhere I shop I see people whom I know—teachers, neighbors, classmates, and relatives. Downtown is bustling. I wish I could put this shopping day into a time capsule and share it with people 40 years from now in 2013.

Our Pay Phone

(January 23, 2013)

I never know when the most insignificant statistic, quote, or conversation will trigger a memory of days gone by in our Oswego, but when the memory hits, the floodgates open, setting off all kinds of recollections that I didn't even know were still kicking around in my head.

That happened recently while I was reading *USA Today*. Their colorful graphics, appropriately named "snapshots" located in the lower left hand corner of each section's first page, give people what they want nowadays from an information source—a quick read.

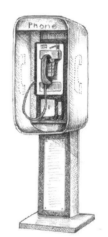

One particular graphic indicated that America is losing yet another icon to the age of technology—the pay phone. In 1999, there were over 2.1 million pay phones in the United States, according to the Federal Communications Commission. Recent estimates say that that number has now dwindled to about 400,000, and the industry is losing about 10 percent every year. It doesn't take a genius to figure out that the pay phone will soon go the way of the 8-track tape and the typewriter.

You're probably thinking: Big deal! Who cares? So what? I know, I know, *everyone* has a cell phone, and most of them do a heck of lot more than make phone calls. You're right. This statistic might have otherwise gone unnoticed, even by a desperate columnist searching for a topic to write about, except it made me think not about the demise of the pay phone in general, but one pay phone in particular—the one on the northwest corner of West Eighth and Bridge Streets in Oswego for most of the 1970s.

Unlike other dinosaurs, there are not even skeletal remains of that pay phone on the corner that used to house the Highway Oil (once known as Workingman's Friend) gas station. The phone, and that corner, were named not for the gas station they were near, but for the across-the-street business, the Oswego Sub Shop. Oswego teens loved "The Sub Shop Corner."

When I was in high school in the early '70s, the malt-shop/soda fountain hangouts popularized in movies about the '50s like *American Graffiti* were largely replaced by house parties. We really didn't have an Arnold's Drive-in like Richie, Potsie, Ralph and the Fonz had on *Happy Days*.

Even worse, we had no Internet or smart phones to network with our friends once we had left home for a night out. So how did we connect with friends to find out where people were heading? Was everyone going to a Laker hockey game at Romney or were someone's parents out of town so we could have a party?

In the absence of a defined social network, we had the pay phone on the corner of West Eighth and Bridge. That pay phone was our social network. Our network wasn't based on hundreds of Facebook friends, but it centered around a ten-cent-per-call pedestal pay phone that stood like a sentry overseeing our comings-and-goings.

I wish I could remember the number. I tried. I figured if I could remember my locker combination from high school (39-19-36, locker #2733), then I might recall the pay phone number, but I can't even remember my kids' current cell numbers, so remembering a solitary phone number from 38 years ago was highly unlikely. I can tell you this though, there were over 400 members of the OHS Class of '75 and I'd wager that more than 300 of us knew that phone number by heart—without today's advancements such as a contacts list or speed dial.

If you're younger than age 45, I'm pretty sure that if you've read this far, you're thinking, "Is this for real? An outdoor pay telephone that almost everyone at OHS knew the number of, and called to see who was hanging out, what was going on, or to catch a ride somewhere." Yeah, it was for real.

Who would answer the phone? Anyone and everyone. We would

walk (another antiquated custom—kids of the '70s walked places—not the cliché "uphill both ways," but we did walk) or be dropped off at the corner and plan from there. In the winter, we planned quickly because Oswego winters were no less harsh in the '70s than they are today.

I guess it's kind of ironic that the decline of the pay phone was on the horizon the same year I graduated from high school, for in 1975, the Motorola Company was granted the first patent for a cellular phone.

At the corner of West Eighth and Bridge Streets, the gas station is closed and the phone is long gone. But the memories remain of a connection to friends, rides, games, parties, and good times. Before *everyone* had a phone, we had *our* phone in our Oswego.

Note: Shortly after this column appeared, Tim Babcock came forward with, believe it or not, the phone number of the famed pay phone at the Sub Shop corner. Apparently, Tim remembers things like obscure phone numbers. When Tim gave me the number, it really didn't ring a bell in my memory, but I tried calling it. The person who answered probably wouldn't appreciate it being published here.

•

Sunday Ritual
(January 22, 2014)

To a Catholic school baby boomer, Sundays were special in Oswego during the 1960s and '70s.

Of course there was Sunday morning Mass, but soon after the final blessing each week, hundreds of people would make their way to the gym at Oswego Catholic High School to watch or play CYO basketball.

CYO basketball was not just another youth sports program in Oswego. It was a Sunday ritual around which families would plan their days. Each Catholic parish had its own team with distinctive school colors. Holy Family and Immaculate Conception represented the Fulton Catholic communities in the league, and by the time I was in eighth grade, Oswego fielded teams from St. Mary's, St. Joseph's, St. John's, St. Peter's, St. Stephen's and St. Paul's.

Since there was not a lot of college basketball on TV in those days, and the month of March was not yet full of "madness," most of us were introduced to sportsmanship, team colors, school spirit, animated coaches, cheerleaders, and hoop rivalries through CYO basketball.

The rivalries were intense. The small gym at St. Francis Hall would be jammed to its arched rafters with parents, classmates and even priests and nuns cheering enthusiastically for their boys. I was never good enough to make the CYO team, so I was one of the supportive fans cheering on my green-and-gold-clad St. Paul's classmates like Patrick Shannon, Mickey Losurdo, Rick Turner, Jimmy Culeton, and Bobby Farrell. Sometimes the crowds were so big, that the overflow fans had to be accommodated in makeshift seating on the stage at the east end of the gymnasium. Maybe it was the acoustics of the gym, but I recall that venue being louder than many of the professional arenas and stadiums I have been in since.

As an eighth grader, I was in a unique situation of divided loyalty. I was a west-sider, living just four blocks from St. Mary's, yet I attended school at St. Paul's—long-time rivals of the blue and white of St. Mary's. Though I was fortunate to have two sets of friends (my neighborhood pals and my school friends), Sundays were difficult, because I rooted for my St. Paul's classmates at the expense of my neighborhood buddies.

I admit that I can't recall the scores of any individual games, an overtime buzzer-beater, or even which parish won the 1971 championship, but I vividly remember the game-day atmosphere—the spirit, the camaraderie, and our post-game trips to Carrol's Restaurant.

Carrol's Corporation is now a Central New York mega-company that owns hundreds of Burger King restaurants, but back in the '70s, Carrol's operated only a handful of locations in the area, and the Oswego franchise was where the St. Paul's players, cheerleaders, and fans went to either celebrate an exciting CYO victory or lament a tough loss.

(Photo courtesy of Carrol's Corporation)

We'd walk the 10 or so blocks from the "Cat High" gym to Carrol's, pushing each other into snow banks, playing keep-away with each other's winter stocking caps, and basically just being rambunctious eighth graders. (For those who don't recall or didn't know the Oswego of 1971, our Carrol's Restaurant, as pictured on the previous page, was located at 169 East Bridge Street, the current location of Monro Muffler.)

On a Sunday afternoon during CYO season, Carrol's was our post-game hangout. It was where we could crowd into their orange booths and be away from parental supervision and the watchful eyes of our teachers. It was just a place where we kids could be kids.

While my friends wolfed down Carrol's iconic Club Burger, my favorite was the Sea Fillet sandwich. No matter what we ordered for food, it seems like everyone ordered the famous "Triple-Thick Shake" to drink.

But it wasn't just about the food. It was about fun and friendship. We'd sit for what seemed like hours, talking, laughing, teasing, and stealing each other's French fries. And as Sunday afternoon turned into Sunday evening, we'd disperse and head home with a day of memories under our belts, ready for a week of school, before repeating the same Sunday routine seven days later.

•

It Suits Me to a 'T'
(October 16, 2013)

Everybody has a favorite t-shirt, whether it bears the Nike swoosh, the logo of a rock band, or the Oswego lighthouse. Though t-shirts are everywhere, have you ever seen a t-shirt claiming, "This shirt is 100 years old?" Probably not, but the t-shirt is believed to be 100 years old this year. According to CustomInk, an online t-shirt vendor, the U.S. Navy issued a light undershirt for sailors to wear under their uniforms, in 1913, thus the t-shirt was born.

I'm writing about t-shirts because Oswego has a significant historical connection to the t-shirt.

In today's world, 98 percent of all men's undershirts are made overseas, mostly in places like China or Thailand; but I recall a time when t-shirts were made and sold about 100 yards from my house. As I've written many times, some of my early Oswego memories come from living at 93 East Seneca Street, in my grandmother's house. I have hundreds of old black and white photos from the early '60s taken near the corner of East 8th and Seneca Streets, and in the background of just about every one of those photos is a large brick building just to the north of gram's house—the Conn Knitting Mill.

Bear with me (or correct me if I'm wrong) because I was a very young child when the Conn Knitting Mill was producing t-shirts for the world, but this is what I think I remember. The factory spanned the width of an entire city block from East Ninth Street to East Eighth. Nowadays, there's a vacant lot on the East Eighth Street side and a large garage facing Ninth Street.

I literally lived two doors down from the mill. I recall a late summer family ritual when Gram (who once worked there) would take my cousins, my brother, and me to the mill for our back-to-school t-shirts. I remember looking into the factory and being amazed by the rows of women at their noisy sewing machines producing t-shirts.

I recall thinking that having the factory right in our backyard was *pretty cool*. I don't know why, but looking back now, I think it was *really cool*. Nowadays, so few products are made in the U.S.A., but back then, I could have not only said that my t-shirts were made in America, or made in New York, but I could have boasted that they were made in Oswego—on my street.

My grandmother used to call the Conn Knitting Mill the "Last-Long." Maybe the name was a holdover from when the Last-Long Underwear Company occupied the factory. But I think they called it the Last-Long because that's what their products did—they lasted a long time. Kids can be rough on clothes, but I seem to remember these t-shirts as being virtually indestructible. It seemed like I only needed new ones when I outgrew the old.

I did some research to jog more memories of the mill. I searched archives from the *Palladium Times* and found hundreds of entries for "Conn Knitting Mill." Apparently, the mill advertised every single day in the Oswego daily newspaper. It was a small, two-inch advertisement, with no pictures or graphics, just bold letters proclaiming:

T-SHIRTS
Shop our outlet store for the best.
Your money will be refunded if you don't think so.
Save the middleman's profit.
CONN KNITTING MILL
110 East 9th Street

Whatever happened to the Last-Long? After the factory closed, and the sewing machines were silenced, the building was used in 1980 by the Oswego Jaycees as a haunted house for Halloween. Near the end of the

'80s it was targeted by developers for renovation. With recent projects in town like the Stevedore and Seaway lofts, I bet that a condo complex would've been a nice fit in that quiet, residential second ward neighborhood, a leisurely stroll from Fort Ontario. But a roof collapse in the fall of 1989 caused the developers to scratch their plans and the building was razed.

Colorful tie-dye t-shirts were symbolic of the counter-culture of the '60s. Maybe the plain, white, well-made Conn Knitting Mill t-shirts were making a social statement of their own, as a metaphor of a bygone era when life was simple, uncomplicated, and of high quality.

It's too bad that the old Conn Knitting Mill closed. With marketing and advertising campaigns what they are in this day-and-age, they could've made a fortune selling t-shirts to Oswego visitors proclaiming, "My parents went to Oswego, NY and all they got me was this Last-Long t-shirt!"

•

The Stamp of Approval
(February 19, 2014)

In today's world, some people justify especially large, unnecessary purchases by accumulating air miles or rewards points through their credit card companies. Spend $1,000 and get cash-back rewards, free plane tickets, or extended hotel stays.

What most consumers under the age of 50 probably don't remember is that there was a similar retail loyalty reward program in place for over a century before our move towards being a cashless society. The program offered consumers free merchandise, and it encouraged shopping in much the same way people use plastic cards today. The incentive to buy came in the form of S & H Green Stamps.

I have some fond (and some not-so-fond) memories of Green Stamps.

I recall shopping with my mom in stores that boldly displayed the green, white, and red signs that proclaimed "We Give   S & H Green Stamps Here."

Not all stores or gas stations gave the stamps, but those that did had loyal customer followings. I remember shopping at the Acme grocery  store on West Second Street and seeing the wheel-like device above the cash register that would dispense the stamps. The cashier would "dial" the amount spent, and this machine would magically (well, it was magic to a child) spit out the corresponding number of stamps. Some stamps were small and some were large (the bigger ones would equal 10 of the smaller stamps), but either way, it would take a value of 50 to fill one of the grid-like pages in the S & H "Quick Saver Book." The small 24-page book would be filled by 1,200 points of stamps.

In my family's kitchen in the '60s, we had a junk drawer that had the usual flashlight batteries, playing cards, a shoe horn, and our cache of Green Stamps. My mom shopped at a lot of local places that awarded Green Stamps, but she was never too keen on placing them in the books and redeeming them.

Once, when I was old enough to figure out that the drawer full of stamps was actually worth something, I negotiated a deal with mom. I told her I would lick all the stamps and put them in the books if I could have them to buy whatever I wanted at the S & H store. I think I was inspired to make this deal with mom by a memorable episode of *The Brady Bunch*. Remember when the six Brady kids decided to combine their resources and cash in their Checker Trading Stamps because the local vendor was going out of business? The battle lines were drawn by gender, as the Brady boys wanted a rowboat and the girls wanted a sewing machine. The always-democratic Brady clan decided to settle the dispute by having the kids build a house of cards to resolve the family dilemma.

Anyway, my mom took my offer and I started licking. Stamp after stamp, book after book. (I guess I was old enough to see the value in the stamps, but not smart enough to think about using a sponge or water to moisten the stamps). Who knows what kind of '60s chemicals these stamps were coated with, but I survived the God-awful taste and was ready to cash in the stamps for all kinds of neat merchandise.

The S & H store in downtown Oswego was nestled between Tot-n-Teen and Burnside Pharmacy in the 200 block of West First Street. There were some miscellaneous items in the store, mostly small appliances like toasters and coffee pots, but they also had a merchandise catalog called the Ideabook. In fact, while doing some research recently, I learned that the S & H rewards catalog was the most circulated publication in the United States in the '60s, with more Ideabooks published than *Life* magazines or *Reader's Digests*.

It was an interesting lesson in economics for a kid looking at the S & H catalog because it didn't have prices in dollars and cents, but it had the cost of merchandise in books and partial books of Green Stamps. For example, a hair dryer might have cost 2½ books, whereas 20 books could be redeemed for a Polaroid Swinger camera.

I'd like to say I redeemed the stamps for a cool prize like a color TV, the same as the Brady kids got, but I honestly can't recall what I left the store with—other than a bad taste in my mouth (literally).

Believe it or not, you can still redeem old S & H Green Stamps. Of course, it's done online, but if you're cleaning out an attic, basement, or junk drawer and discover a stash of the stamps, you can get $1.20 for every completed book. It's not enough to fund your retirement, but just finding these treasures might be valuable in the memories they bring back. Just don't ask me to help you lick the stamps.

•

The Spirits of Breitbeck

(May 28, 2014)

I recently read that earlier this month (May 3) was "Love Your Park Day," an initiative of the New York State legislature encouraging New Yorkers to get out and contribute time to clean, enhance, and at the very least, enjoy their favorite state parks.

I missed celebrating that statewide event, but with Memorial Day and warmer weather here, it's actually a better time to celebrate and enjoy a park. I usually head to a nearby state park (Southwick or Fair Haven) a few times a summer, and have had some great times at Wellesley Island State Park in the Thousand Islands region. But my favorite park, the park that I truly love, is not a state park, but a city park—Breitbeck.

With all due respect to the organizers of Harborfest, I enjoy Breitbeck much more on a quiet spring weekday than on the last weekend in July. During Harborfest, the real beauty of Breitbeck is masked by vendors, barricades, crowds, and noise.

But on quieter days, I enjoy walking Breitbeck Park with what I call the spirits of Breitbeck. No, I don't channel the departed Rosemary Nesbitt for a reading of "Tales of the Haunted Harbor" (though there is a fantastic monument to Mrs. Nesbitt near the Breitbeck bell).

Instead, the ghosts of Breitbeck with whom I walk are those whose families have placed memorial benches along the park's promenade. I can't help but glance at the engraved plaques that are mounted on so many of the park's benches overlooking the lake. I think what first drew me to these memorials was the fact that so many of the names were familiar to me from growing up in the first ward, just two blocks from Breitbeck. There's a bench dedicated to my old neighbor on West Schuyler Street, Joseph A. Losurdo. I saw his son Dick walking in the park a few weeks back, and he echoed what the bench to his dad reads: "He loved to look out upon this lake everyday."

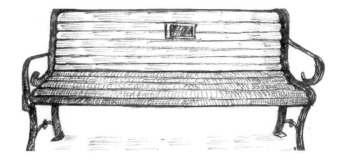

The Lowery family, whom I knew well through lots of sandlot ball games with Jack and Bob, dedicated a bench to their parents Joseph and Mary. Their inscription simply invites people to enjoy a magnificent sunset in remembrance of their parents.

I walk with the spirits of first ward residents Ray and Lillian McCloskey. As a kid, I recall seeing Mr. McCloskey walking the park with his dogs for many years.

My childhood friends the Muldoons have memorialized their dad, Tom, who, as his bench reads, was not only a lover of the lake, but a proud veteran and avid sailor.

Other benches are dedicated to loved ones who passed away much too young. Michael DelSavio was only a teenager when he perished in a surfing accident on the big Island of Hawaii in 1994. I didn't know Mike, but I learned all of this about him from reading his bench.

Mike Boyzuick, Sr., who passed away last year has a dedicated bench overlooking the lake. How appropriate it is that his bench is a great place to sit and fly a kite.

The King "kids," who are no longer kids, chose to honor their "amazing mom" through a bench with an inscription expressing their hopes that others enjoy the park and view as much as their mom did.

Dominic and Dorothy D'Amore's family, whom my own parents knew well, are memorialized with an attractive bench near the park pavilion.

There are, of course, many others, living and deceased, who are honored with a beautiful bench with an even more beautiful view. My old neighbor Mrs. Zetta Hawley, who lived in the "haunted house" as we kids called it, on the corner of West 8th and Van Buren streets has a bench, as do Alice Fitzpatrick Mitchell, Francis "Bomber" Weigelt, Charles & Teresa Walters, Addie Stevens, the Ross family, Maynard & Clara Fletcher, Willard "Will Eye" Corbett, Ron & Betty Clary, and many more.

There are other tribute benches in various places around town that I always stop and read. West Linear Park, near the Veterans' Memorial, has several benches with memorial inscriptions to those who served our country. The Community Walkway around Glimmerglass Lagoon at SUNY Oswego is lined with tribute benches as well, many to Oswego citizens who fostered college-community relations.

One of my favorites is the one dedicated by the OHS Class of 1955 at the west end of the Harbor Rail Trail. I wonder how many Oswegonians in their 70s sit and reminisce while gazing at the Harbor House Condominiums, the building in which so many of their high school memories were made 60 years ago.

They say one of the best things about retirement is that you can stop to smell the roses. But when I'm out and about in an Oswego park, I like to stop to read the benches. I can't think of a better way to show your love for a park or to honor a friend or family member, than with a memorial like this.

Note: Since this column appeared, several more benches have sprung up on the outer perimeter of Breitbeck Park according to the unofficial "Mayor of Breitbeck," Shirlee Healy, who has her own bench, courtesy of her children on the occasion of her 80th birthday.

●

"We all Scream for Ice Cream"

(July 10, 2013)

There's nothing like ice cream on a hot July night.

Though Oswego has more tattoo parlors, dollar stores, and pizza shops than ice cream places, we still have a nice variety from which we can get a cone, a sundae, or a banana split.

A week from Sundae (excuse the pun, I mean Sunday), July 21, is National Ice Cream Day. (Yeah, it seems like there's a national day for everything.) But why not celebrate with a cold confection from one of your favorite places we currently have in town. We have year-round stand-bys like Friendly's, Stone's, Byrne Dairy, Cold Stone, and others. Or we have seasonal favorites Bev's and PJ's, where there are often long lines, but it's always worth the wait.

But I'm thinking back to a time when we didn't go get our favorite ice cream, but our favorite ice cream came to us in the Mister Softee truck.

Before I became a "west-sider" for life, as an eight year-old, I lived at the corner of East Eighth and Seneca Streets—a quiet second ward neighborhood just a stone's throw from Fort Ontario. Other than the corner store a block away, I'm not sure where the nearest ice cream establishment was in the mid '60s. I do recall though, that when the half-gallon of Sealtest ice cream was gone from the freezer, there was no more welcome sight than the Mister Softee truck heading north on East Eighth Street.

Thinking back, I have vivid recollections of the Mister Softee experience appealing to several of my five senses. I see a huge, brightly lit white-over-blue truck with the iconic Mister Softee logo emblazoned on all four sides. The colors seemed even more brilliant when contrasting with the dark summer night, for our section of the street was not well lit.

And to a young child, the sight of the ice cream man himself was amazing. He didn't *represent* Mister Softee, he *was* Mister Softee, almost as if he didn't have a real name, and his social security card read "Softee, Mister!" Dressed all in white, he'd park the truck, move from the cab to the serving window, and slide open the glass like a one-man band.

As striking as the visual image is in my mind, the sounds of the Mister Softee truck were music to my ears. Hearing the melodies of the truck as it approached (the same tune over-and-over-and-over again) set off a chain reaction of events in the house. My brother and I would rush to porch to verify that he was indeed heading our way. Next, we'd plead with mom to buy ice cream for us. Then, mom would inevitably scramble to find money in her purse, and finally, we'd begin negotiations about the size and cost of the treat as we headed out the door to the curb. My opening appeal to mom was usually a large vanilla milk shake, and her counter-proposal was a small cone. We'd often compromise with a medium cone, but on a good night, if the grown-ups had already partaken in some of their own after-dinner beverages (Genesee beer), sprinkles would be a bonus for us kids.

(I'm not sure when someone decided to crush up candy and throw it in with ice cream, inventing the Flurry, Frenzy, Blizzard, etc., but I can only imagine how those concoctions would've complicated matters in 1965 at the window of the Mister Softee truck!)

Though the sights and sounds of my memory have been reawakened thinking of Mister Softee, they pale in comparison to the taste of the ice cream treats. Maybe everything tasted better in the 1960s, but I've literally tried truckloads of ice cream in the decades since, yet those medium Mister Softee cones that melted down my arms on hot summer nights are still my favorites.

I haven't seen a Mister Softee truck in Oswego for a very long time, but it is still a viable company, based in New Jersey, using the original truck designs, music, logos, and recipes from the old days.

I've been retired for a year now and haven't quite discovered my "encore career." Maybe I'll look into a Mister Softee franchise. I'd likely be my own best customer.

•

The Neighborhood Store
(August 21, 2013)

All of us have probably shopped at a department store, a super center, or a convenience store recently, but when's the last time we thought about the old neighborhood store?

I miss those stores that were sprinkled throughout Oswego neighborhoods in the 1960s. They probably should've been called convenience stores, but that name seemed reserved for all of the stores with gas stations attached that dominate our cityscape today.

Those neighborhood stores of bygone days were very convenient. They were convenient to stay-at-home moms (most moms were stay-at-home moms in the '60s) who had to walk a block or two to the store for some eggs or flour or whatever, because dad had driven the one-and-only family car to work.

But these stores were most convenient to us kids who would take a break from playing outdoors in the summer sun for some good, old-fashioned junk food. The corner store provided the five major "food groups" we sought: pop (we never called it "soda"), Slim Jims, Popsicles (the double, two-stick Popsicle of the '60s that mom made me break in half and share with my little brother), Twinkies, and penny candy.

Since I had (and still have) an insatiable sweet tooth, the penny candy display was always my favorite. Items that will send me to my dentist for a damaged crown, or to my doctor for a diverticulitis flare up nowadays, were the most appealing to me in the 1960s. I loved jawbreakers, Turkish taffy, candy necklaces, and red hot dollars. The store owners usually knew us and our parents, so they'd often throw in an extra piece of candy, enabling us to leave the store with a small brown paper bag full of goodies for only a quarter.

It's amazing looking back, but these small stores that were often converted homes from the previous generation, seemed to have inventories as vast as today's 200,000 square foot big box super centers. I can never recall the proprietors of these stores saying, "We're all out of candy," or "Tell your mom that this week's *Life* magazine is on back order."

Unlike the cookie-cutter convenience stores of today, the neighborhood stores seemed to have personalities of their own.

Of course, there were many common traits. You could spot the stores a block away with their hinged porcelain signs protruding from the buildings, usually emblazoned with a Coca-Cola logo along with the store owner's family name. I also remember creaky wooden floors in most, and the obligatory bell above the door that jingled to alert the shopkeeper of customers entering.

The merchants were our neighbors—always familiar faces—not some management trainee sent from corporate headquarters. I seem to recall them as either little old men or little old ladies, but as I reflect, the harsh reality is that I'm probably older now than those store owners were back then.

I spent some time recently with my friend Ed Stacy trying to recall as many of these stores as we could, their locations, and their owners. I apologize, in advance, for leaving out some of the businesses from the good ole days, but as kids, we didn't get all over town—only as far as our bikes would take us.

In a four block radius around my grandmother's second ward home were three nearby stores: Pat McCarthy's (East 7th and Seneca), Spano's (East 9th and Schuyler), and Russo's (East 10th and Seneca). And that's not even mentioning Carson's News and Garafolo's a few blocks to the south on Bridge Street. I remember Piazza's, Ure's, Pagano's, and of course the surviving Bosco & Geers on the east side, south of Bridge Street, but they weren't quite walking distance for seven-year-old me to patronize.

Castrogiovanni's Market at the corner of West Eighth and Utica Streets was more of an all-purpose market than a neighborhood store, but the convenience and small-store atmosphere were a stark contrast to today's super centers.

After my family moved to the west side, our closest neighborhood stores were Skillen's (West Schuyler between 7th and 8th) and Amedio's on the corner of Liberty and West Schuyler Streets.

West 5th Street seemed to be a main corridor for neighborhood storefronts. Al's was a block from the hospital on 5th and Oneida, and McConkey's and Lombardo's were across-the-street competitors at West 5th and Albany before a fire razed Lombardo's in the midst of the Blizzard of '66. Bill's Grocery (West 5th and Erie), Lil's (neighboring Kingsford Park school to the south), and Mary's (West 5th and Tallman) took care of the shopping needs of fifth and seventh ward residents.

The Sayer family, of course, operated its store along the river on West 1st Street where Murray Street and Route 48 converge.

There were plenty of other places that could technically fit into a discussion of neighborhood establishments of the past from bakeries (Mahunik's, Meeker's, and Matott's), to small grocery stores (Loblaws, Acme, A & P, Miner's, Castrogiovanni's, IGA, and Utica Cash Market), to newsstands (Fred's to the east and Lupe's to the west).

So the next time you're wandering around a big box store, struggling to find the simplest necessities, you might ask yourself what I wonder every time I'm lost in the aisles at Wal-Mart—is the super center really that super, or was the corner store super in its own way.

•

Playgrounds Were Dangerous and Fun!

(July 23, 2014)

I came to a conclusion the other day that playground equipment ain't what it used to be.

I am amused by the safe playgrounds of today compared to what we played on as kids. Today's playground apparatus look like they were designed by a bunch of wimps with a team of lawyers forbidding them from dreaming up any playground equipment that might lead to a potential lawsuit.

Modern-day playground slides, for instance, are either enclosed, twisty, plastic tubes or they are about as tall as a speed bump. I'm sure two year-olds might enjoy them, but where's the thrill and excitement of climbing a dozen steps up a metal ladder, anticipating a quick return to the ground, down a steep stainless steel slide that is hot enough to fry an egg on. In the playgrounds of my youth, if the metal slides weren't fast enough, we'd accelerate the process with a block of paraffin wax or a sheet of wax paper—both easily "borrowed" from mom's pantry. The sheet of wax paper, strategically placed under one's butt, would turn a trip down the slide into a '60s thrill ride.

If going down the slide in a traditional, feet-first mode wasn't exhilarating enough, we'd try our best Pete Rose head-first slide. The real thrill seekers in my neighborhood weren't content just descending the slide, they'd try running *up* it—not on the ladder-like steps, but on the metal slide itself. It was a challenge, but if the daredevil was unsuccessful and gravity won out, there were some nasty tumbles to the ground.

Slides interest me because of an incident in my own childhood, when my knee was ripped open on a jagged edge at the bottom of a large metal slide. After a trip to the hospital and twenty stitches from my dad's friend Dr. Jerry Belden, I was back on the playground in a few weeks with a life-long scar as a badge of honor.

Walking Oswego's parks recently, I noticed that there's almost no modern-day playground equipment that will induce dizziness or vomiting like some of our favorites from days gone by.

In my neighborhood, for a while we had playground equipment at the Diamond Match Park and at Sundown Park (the original name of Breitbeck Park before it was renamed after first ward alderman George Breitbeck). Two of our favorites were the merry-go-round and the maypole. To a child nowadays, a merry-go-ground induces an image of calliope music and horses slowly moving in a circular pattern. No, no, no! That's a carousel. Our merry-go-rounds were lessons in physics and inertia. The apparatus was a large metal circle that was only about a foot off the ground. It could be propelled in a couple of ways. Usually, the riders would start it by grasping the bars and running around it before jumping aboard. Then, a smarter neighborhood kid, with feet firmly planted on the ground, would continue spinning it while the rest of us would beg for mercy while hanging on for dear life.

What we kids called a maypole, my cousins called a witch's hat. Their label did seem more fitting because this piece of playground equipment really did resemble the pointed triangular hat of a witch. Its brim was a metal circle that we would grasp, with our teeth clenched and feet dangling, as someone spun us until we couldn't take it anymore and let go, as we crashed dizzily to earth.

Back in the day, crashing to earth meant falling onto really hard ground—not wood chips or a synthetic rubberized shock-absorbing surface underfoot to ease the blow and prevent broken bones. In later years, the safest surface we landed on was composed of little pebbles to break our fall. (Those pebbles also made a cool sound when someone would throw a handful of them at the spinning metal merry-go-round filled with friends.)

Good, old-fashioned monkey bars may have been stationary, but they were no less dangerous to us baby boom kids than the moving equipment. These steel mazes, probably painted with classic lead paint of the '60s, were a place to climb, sit and talk, and even attempt an unsupervised chin-up or upside-down hang.

Even today's swings are safer than those of bygone days. We would pump our legs on the swings to a height that would give us a second of weightlessness before gravity swung us backward. And how many times did we launch ourselves off the swings trying to set a flying long jump record just like 1968 Olympic hero Bob Beamon did?

Another standby at our neighborhood playgrounds was the teeter-totter. Some kids called it a see-saw, but it was the same basic premise. Our teeter-totters were big wooden boards, maybe 2x6 or 2x8 planks. My chiropractor is probably still correcting damage done on the teeter totter when one of my "buddies" jumped off while I was suspended 6 feet in the air playing "Farmer, farmer let me down" and the "What will you give me" response wasn't enough!

I'm not criticizing today's safe playgrounds. I just have fond memories of the days when playgrounds were less safe, but more fun.

•

Hijinks at Hollis

(August 6, 2014)

In 1975, *M*A*S*H* was among the top-rated shows on network television. That's the same year that I was hired as a counselor at Camp Hollis.

What do these two, seemingly unrelated facts have in common? Working that summer at Camp Hollis was just like being a cast member in the popular sitcom. I'm not sure which cast member I was like. I never wore women's clothes, so I certainly wasn't Corporal Klinger, and I didn't have powers of clairvoyance, so I wasn't the bespectacled Radar O'Reilly.

The parallels between *M*A*S*H* and Camp Hollis came not from me, but from two of my bunkmates Sanford J. (Sandy) MacMillen and Rich Henry. To me, a naïve seventeen-year-old, they weren't just similar to the fictional TV cut-ups Captain Benjamin Franklin Pierce and Captain John McIntyre, they *were* Hawkeye and Trapper.

These two co-workers were a little older, and a lot more worldly-wise than I. Like the pair of army surgeons from *M*A*S*H*, Sandy and Rich had larger-than-life personalities, that remain memorable to me all these years later. Both of them had a fantastic sense of humor. Whether devising irreverent nicknames for the Camp Director (I guess she would've been cast as the Margaret "Hot Lips" Houlihan of the staff), or entertaining the young Camp Hollis residents, their humor prevailed.

Kids who attended Camp Hollis returned home with many fond memories and a t-shirt displaying this iconic camp logo.

I can still see Sandy walking, half-awake in his bathrobe and shower shoes towards the flagpole for the morning Pledge of Allegiance exactly like Hawkeye answered the reveille call in the long-running TV comedy.

After the first week on staff, I got up enough courage to ask Sandy about the nickname he called Rich--"Ming T. Merciless." I knew the character Ming from the old black and white "Flash Gordon" reruns, but it certainly didn't fit Rich's easy-going demeanor. So I simply asked, "What does the 'T' stand for?" His reply was simply the word "The." As he laughed and went about this business, I scratched my head and muttered to myself "Ming The Merciless." (I was expecting a much deeper meaning!)

As hilarious as they were antagonistic to authority (à la Hawkeye and Trapper), their most endearing trait was their genuine concern for the kids. Back then, Camp Hollis was a week-long summer camp experience primarily for children from lower-income Oswego County families. I learned a lot of things from Sandy and Rich, including a shortcut from Camp Hollis down the beach to Nunzi's and an appreciation for the music of the Moody Blues. But the most unforgettable lesson I learned from them was that many of these kids needed an adult who cared about them. So, for eight one-week sessions, we were their caregivers. In addition to the obvious food and shelter the county camp provided, we hiked, swam, played basketball, and sung around the campfire with the young campers.

The highlight of each week was the final evening's legendary dance, "The Hollis Hop." The female counselors would prepare the girls for the event in their wing of the bunkhouse, and we would do the same with the boys. I'm not sure what the female staff did to get the girls "all gussied up," but we introduced the boys to manly fragrances.

We male counselors would bring a bottle of "vintage" cologne or after-shave to camp each week. I didn't do much shaving as a seventeen year-old, but I do recall cleaning out my dad's medicine cabinet to bring in bottles of Brut, English Leather, and Hai Karate that I'm pretty sure had been fermenting since LBJ was president a decade before.

In a rite of passage, the boys would cup their hands and splash on the masculine colognes. Like Macaulay Culkin depicted years later in the box office hit *Home Alone*, there were lots of peach-fuzzed-cheeks stinging, as they splashed on Aqua Velva or Old Spice for the first time.

Imagine the doors to the dining room-turned-dance-hall-for-the-evening opening up and 40-50 pre-pubescent boys strutting into the room, sporting a mixture of aromatic fragrances from days gone by. I don't know what a French brothel smells like, but I'm willing to bet that it may have smelled something like the Friday night Hollis Hops of '75.

Several generations of Oswego County kids who attended Camp Hollis have fond memories of their week at camp—and based on my experiences, so do the staff members. Remembering my summer job at the camp is like watching a rerun of M*A*S*H—it always brings a smile to my face.

•

Backyard Carnivals
(September 3, 2014)

As I sat at a stoplight last Saturday at the Forks in the Road, I saw an Oswego firefighter approach with boot in hand. Of course I recognized the annual voluntary toll set up by the OFD to raise both funds and awareness for the Muscular Dystrophy Association.

For some reason, that firefighter triggered an almost fifty-year-old memory in me for the same cause. How many of us kids of the '60s, held backyard carnivals for the MDA?

I had a couple such fundraisers when I was a kid, but the memories blend together, so I had to supplement my recollections with a little modern-day research.

Back then, the backyard carnivals were heavily publicized around the country on local kids' TV shows that were all the rage in that era. The TV personality usually dressed up as a silly character and introduced cartoons in front of a live studio audience. The local celebrity would also make appearances at stores and strip malls, and in late spring, would heavily promote the backyard carnivals for "Jerry's kids."

Two such TV hosts in the Syracuse television market (remember, we only had channels 3, 5, and 9) were Denny Sullivan and Bill Everett. We knew Everett better as "Salty Sam." His on-camera persona entertained an entire generation of Central New York kids on WSYR channel 3, and taught kids about the spirit of volunteerism by encouraging us to host carnivals for Muscular Dystrophy.

Remember the process? Kids would send away for a Carnival Kit that included everything from suggestions for games and events to posters to nail on every telephone pole in the neighborhood.

I hosted a couple carnivals in the '60s, but the promotion lasted well into the 1970s. If you sent to channel 3 for a Carnival Kit, you weren't alone. In 1972, Central New York kids hosted 700 backyard carnivals. That was on the heels of a productive 1971, when nationwide, 22,000 carnivals were held, raising over $500,000.

Some of the kids who raised the most money in Central New York were even rewarded with a TV appearance, where they would hand their profits over to Salty Sam himself. We never raised enough to gain such celebrity, but after our carnivals, we counted the change (and an occasional dollar bill) from the cigar box that we had used as a cash box. After mom went to the bank for a money order, we dutifully sent our proceeds to the Syracuse TV station.

The games at our carnivals reflected the simplicity of the times. Toss a penny on to a plate and bobbing for apples were two of the old standbys. The bake sale and lemonade stand always proved profitable. I vividly recall the buzz one of our carnivals created with a brand new outdoor game that my dad bought just for the event—Jarts.

Looking back, Jarts had to be one of the most dangerous toys ever invented. They were giant dart-like projectiles with large, sharp metal tips. You played Jarts like horseshoes. The object of the game was to toss your Jarts into, or closest to, the plastic ring that was always precariously placed near your opponents' feet some fifteen or twenty yards away.

There is no doubt about the dangers Jarts presented as a lawn game, but the novelty of them, unveiled for the first time at our backyard carnival, made them an instant hit and a great money maker. I think we awarded some type of prize to the kid who finished with the most ringers without having his foot pierced by a Jart.

This newspaper's archives are filled with news briefs and personals on the local page about Oswego County kids hosting MDA carnivals. An August 12, 1971 article said that the Micelis on East River Road made $12.33. Tracey, Tammy, and Trisha Cary along with Shelley Knopp, Leslie Resnick, and Mike Lavery are pictured at their carnival that raised $39.58 in the August 3, 1973 *Palladium-Times*. And with Tammy Buskey as the ringmaster, the kids from the North Road in Scriba raised $112, as reported on August 12, 1974.

I certainly don't recall how much the McCrobie kids raised at our backyard carnivals, but the amounts are far less important than the lessons that were learned. Many kids of the '60s and '70s learned compassion, generosity and philanthropy that have become a part of their adult lives through the humble beginnings of hosting a backyard carnival for Jerry's kids.

•

The Railroad Bridge Incident
(September 17, 2014)

One of the nicest routes for a leisurely stroll in Oswego is over the Harbor Rail Trail, the quarter-mile promenade that joins the east and west sides between the busy Utica Street and Bridge Street thoroughfares.

Many of us, however, recall a time when crossing that expanse wasn't a leisurely stroll, but a mad dash. You see, for the current generation, it's the Harbor Rail Trail, but for many of us, it will always be known as the railroad bridge. Back in the day, you often had to hustle across the railroad bridge to beat a train that was either gaining on you from behind, or coming at you like, well, like a speeding locomotive!

Looking eastward from the railroad bridge, circa 1960, the O & W tunnel, the courthouse and Cyclotherm are in the background.

Many 50+ Oswegonians can recall stories of a close encounter of some kind on the railroad bridge, most likely from their teenage years.

I don't have any recollections of railroad bridge dares from my high school days, but I remember hearing my parents tell a story many times about my first trip over the bridge.

Apparently, I was about six years old, and my brother was three. We lived on the east side at the time, and one summer day, our baby sitter decided to take us to visit our mom, who was working at city hall. Now, I probably shouldn't reveal our baby sitter's name, but I can't resist. Her name was Margie Woods at that time; now she's Margie Pollard. (She's knows this is coming, but she's probably going to be mad at me anyway!)

For some reason, our then-teenage baby sitter, thought it would be a good idea to take me, on foot, and my brother, in his stroller, over the railroad bridge.

Obviously, we made it safely across the bridge that day without incident to visit mom at work, and kept our secret when we got to city hall as our baby sitter requested: "Don't tell your mother we walked over the railroad bridge." I should say, I kept the secret until later that night, when six-year-old me probably said something like, "We had fun walking over the train bridge with Margie today!"

That's when all hell broke loose. The cat was out of the bag. I remember bits and pieces of this for two reasons. First, the story was told over and over again in family lore by adults who were old enough to remember the infamous "Railroad Bridge Incident." Secondly, because it was the first recollection I have of my mom being mad. Really mad. Let's face it, most parents, whether in 1963 or 2014, probably wouldn't be thrilled with the idea of their two small children walking an arm's length away from an oncoming 90-ton locomotive high above a raging river.

I'm not sure what happened next, but those of us who eventually became parents or grandparents can likely fill in the details. Probably a phone call at the very least. Maybe a visit right to Margie's home a few blocks from ours. I don't remember a lot of shouting or swearing (but knowing my full-blooded Irish mom, there was probably plenty of both).

There were no serious repercussions that I was aware of. I'm sure that Margie continued to be our baby sitter for several more years to come, but I'm equally positive that it was our final trip over the railroad bridge as toddlers.

I've talked to a lot of people recently who remember the daredevil nature of a walk over the railroad bridge. They recall the sight of the oncoming train either as it emerged from the tunnel heading west, or as it crossed the West First and Utica Street intersection when it was eastbound. Lots of Oswego folks remember the sound of the warning whistle and even the rumbling of the locomotive on the rails and planks beneath their feet.

It seems silly that with two other bridges, with safe, concrete sidewalks only a short distance away, that people young and old would risk a walk across the railroad bridge, but whether it was on a challenge from a friend, a task for pledging a fraternity or sorority, or just for an adrenaline rush, it was a rite of passage for many Oswegonians.

•

5

SCHOOL DAYS

Did You Hear They Stole the Regents?
(June 11, 2014)

I've written before about the so-called "Where were you when you heard the news" moments in my lifetime—JFK's assassination, the Challenger space shuttle explosion, and 9/11.

But we're approaching the anniversary of a moment that was far less tragic, but equally memorable to high school students forty years ago this month.

Where were you, in 1974, when you heard that the Regents exams were stolen?

I was a high school junior in June of '74, and though I was a good student, the thought of taking four three-hour Regents exams was daunting. I was scheduled to take the state exams in Chemistry, Trigonometry, English, and American History. And though my teachers Vinnie Savona, Margaret Wales, Margaret Bernardi, and Charlie Young respectively had prepared me well in these courses, it was still a tense time with class rank, college acceptances, and the coveted Regents Diploma riding on the scores.

So, where was I when I heard "the news?" Remember, in those days, students didn't get text messages or receive automated "robo" calls; we got our information from the news. I was working my part-time job as a dishwasher at Auyer's Silver Skillet (now the Ritz Diner) on West First Street. It was a Friday night, so the diner was busy with customers enjoying Dick Auyer's fish fry. Since the diner was hopping, so was the 16-year-old kid washing dishes.

In the midst of loading the dishwasher and scouring pots and pans, I heard part of a news broadcast on the portable radio that we had on the shelf above the sink, tucked in between Brillo pads and dishwashing liquid.

The radio reporter said something about stolen Regents exams in New York City. He continued with sketchy details using phrases like "compromised the exam's security" and "possible cancellation." While scrubbing baked-on macaroni and cheese from pans, I thought, "Man, are those New York City kids lucky to have their Regents cancelled."

As the evening wore on, the Oswego rumor mill was kicking into high gear. Patrons would come into the diner with bits and pieces they had heard on the six o'clock TV news, and the waitresses would relay the information to the kitchen help, though Helen, the sixty-year-old cook was much less interested in news about Regents exams than I was.

By the time I got home from work, smelling like grease from the deep fryer, my parents had fielded a couple calls from my friends. (No cell phones, no answering machine, just real land-line telephone calls.) If you know my high school friends like Sam Natoli, Jerry Brown, and Terry Johnson, they had already jumped to conclusions about the test news and told me to forget about studying because all the Regents were going to be cancelled.

I've always been a skeptic, so I needed more proof. Those Friday night rumors persisted into Saturday morning with more speculation, but no verification. But the rumors were soon confirmed and students' dreams came true with a newspaper headline that read "Security Breech Causes Regents Cancellation."

To many, the feeling of relief was better than a snow day announcement in January. On that June Sunday morning, the Alleluia Chorus rang out not only in churches throughout the state, but in the hearts and minds of thousands of anxious high school students. The phone rang all day and friends stopped by the house, giddy with the news that we would not have to endure twelve excruciating hours of Regents exams in the coming week.

As happy as I was to avoid the stress of the tests, I felt a tinge of sadness for my eleventh grade Trigonometry teacher, Miss Wales. She was a great educator who believed in the old saying, "Strive for perfection, and if you must, you may settle for excellence." You see, from the first day of classes in September that year, until the final day of Regents review in June, Miss Wales told us that she not only wanted, but *expected* everyone in the class to get a perfect 100 on the Trig Regents. After learning formulas and equations from her, and hearing her expectations of us for 180 school days, many of us believed that we would indeed get a perfect score on that exam.

We'll never know what we would've scored on those cancelled exams or if the grades would've changed things in our lives such as our college choices or career paths. I do know that I certainly couldn't pass a Trig test today. In fact, I have no idea how forty years have added up since that "Where were you when you heard the news" moment in June of 1974.

•

The Handwriting's on the Wall-or is it?
(September 18, 2013)

The handwriting has been on the wall for years, and it appears that so-called advancements in education are killing off another important aspect of our culture—cursive writing.

Cursive writing is fading away like decades-old ink in my OHS *Paradox* yearbook.

Learning cursive was always a write of passage for early elementary students. (Sorry, I had to use the wrong "rite" as a lame attempt at humor!)

For some, learning cursive was painful, for others, it was a breeze. My memories of cursive writing begin in Sister Elizabeth's third grade classroom at St. Paul's. (She and Mrs. McElhone must have had the patience of saints to teach third graders cursive writing!) I can still see the green cards with perfectly formed white letters, affixed above the blackboard, illustrating the cursive alphabet from a to z in both upper and lower case letters. I recall practicing page after page of letters for homework on that wide-lined tablet paper that had the dotted line in the middle to guide the size of the letters, so the capitals didn't get too big and the lower case letters didn't get too small.

I had my doubts about cursive from the beginning. I remember wondering about the design of some of the letters. Why was the capital "Q" a "2" ? Why do you dot a lower case "i" and "j," but not any other letters? And I could never figure out why the girls in the class had better handwriting than their male counterparts. I wondered if cursive writing was a "girl thing" like playing with Barbies, wearing pink, and screaming at the sight of a frog.

When trying to learn handwriting from the Catholic school nuns a generation before me, my mother's Irish temper likely put the "curse" in cursive. You see, mom was left-handed. After frustrating her teachers and herself trying to form letters from the "other side," the nuns tried to make her write right-handed, almost as if being a lefty was the devil's handiwork. Mom persevered though, learned cursive, remained a southpaw, and to this day, some of my most cherished mementos are cards and notes she wrote to me in her distinctive penmanship.

People fighting to keep cursive alive in schools today claim that it's a form of art. I agree. As a parochial school kid in the 1960s, we didn't have an art teacher, so the cursive alphabet was about as artsy as we ever got. My handwriting was not nearly as elegant as some of my St. Paul's classmates like Jean Canale or Mary Boysman, but it was a series of continuous loops and curlicues. It was fairly readable and reasonably artistic in my eyes.

Since 2010, 45 states have adopted the Common Core standards, the latest "flavor-of-the-month" in education. These standards do not mandate cursive writing instruction in schools, but instead, leave the teaching of cursive up to each state. To me, this is a big mistake. I know educators are supposed to prepare students for the future, but how about preparing them to understand and appreciate the past? How are kids going to read The Declaration of Independence if they can't even write their own John Hancock in cursive? How are people going to trace family trees and ancestry records if they can't tell the difference between a capital F and a capital T?

Just a couple months ago, in the George Zimmerman trial, a witness was asked to read a letter that was a key piece of evidence. On the stand, under oath, she looked at the handwritten letter, lowered her head and said, somewhat humiliated, "I don't read cursive."

I understand that people communicate differently in 2013. I know what Skype is, and I send hundreds of text messages every month. I've heard of Vine, Snapchat, Twitter, Instagram, and hashtags, but I couldn't tell you what any of them are if my life depended on it. Heck, my mother-in-law even has a Facebook account. But my point is this: There's still something special about getting a letter or note, beautifully handwritten in the Palmer Method, from my Aunt Barbara, delivered by the good old-fashioned U.S. Postal Service.

I know it seems hypocritical of me to bemoan the loss of cursive writing, when you're reading something that was keyboarded and typeset for a book, but believe me, the first draft of every piece in this book, was done in cursive writing with pen and paper.

●

Second to Nun

(December 26, 2012)

Have you ever been hustled in dice, poker, or a game of pool? Lots of us have, but I'm willing to bet that I'm in a very small minority of people who have been swindled in a game of eight-ball by a Roman Catholic nun.

In the pre-video game world of 1969, I received two coveted Christmas gifts—a yearbook from the recently crowned World Champion New York Mets and a small pool table that took up nearly the entire living room in our tiny apartment. After honing our billiards skills most of Christmas vacation, my brother and I got the word from mom: "You two need to go outside and play. That pool table will still be here when you come in!"

Begrudgingly, we put on layers of long johns, sweatshirts, snow pants, and gloves and went outdoors to go sledding. When we came back inside, we couldn't believe our eyes. There, bent over our new pool table, going head-to-head in a game of eight-ball, were two of our teachers from St. Paul's Academy. They had just stopped by the apartment to bring my mother a Christmas gift because mom used to do some typing for them. Apparently, they couldn't resist trying their hand at pool.

This vivid childhood memory isn't in the psychedelic, tie-dye colors of the '60s, but it's engraved in my mind in black-and-white—as in the black-and-white of nuns' habits of the era. That's right, my teachers who were visiting on Christmas vacation, playing pool, were not Mr. Caldwell in his Nehru jacket or Miss Spaman in a mini-skirt, but two Roman Catholic nuns in full habits. Sister Ann and Sister Elizabeth were always considered to be "the cool nuns," but seeing them playing pool in our living room, crucifixes dangling with every shot they took, was surreal.

The only thing more bizarre than seeing them play pool, was them challenging my brother and me to a game. If my brother and I won, I would get a guaranteed 100 percent on the next spelling test, Sister

Elizabeth promised. If they won, I'd have to clean the blackboard erasers, outside, after school, the week following vacation. (Clapping the erasers was actually a fun thing to do in the halcyon days of September, but in the midst of an Oswego winter, it was a task usually reserved for the troublemakers.)

We got to break, and it was game on. My brother scattered the balls, but none went in. "No problem," I thought, until Sister Ann confidently lined up a striped ball and buried it in the side pocket. With deliberate backward draws of the cue and smooth thrusts forward, she did the same to *all* of the remaining striped balls—in succession. Before we knew what hit us, the eight ball was falling into the corner pocket and the game was over. They ran the table without giving us a second shot!

How did this happen? Through the wonder years eyes of a twelve-year-old, I envisioned a secret room in the convent where sisters retreated for hours, honing their billiards skills. Or maybe it was Divine intervention? What I do know is that it was a cold week in January when school resumed for me to clap the erasers outside of St. Paul's School.

To this day, when I see a pool table, I don't think of billiards legends like Minnesota Fats or Steve Mizerak. I flash back to a black-and-white image of the day I got hustled in a game of pool by a couple of nuns.

•

"Did You Remember Your Lunch Box?"
(February 20, 2013)

Some crossword puzzle enthusiasts may know that a paleontologist is one who studies fossils. But I'm willing to guess that few know what a "pail-eontologist" is. You can look it up, but it's not really a word.

Pail-eontologists themselves made up the bad pun to describe themselves as participants in one of the fastest-growing and most lucrative collecting hobbies in the country—the collecting of what kids of the '60s called lunch pails.

Last year, while eating lunch in the faculty room at Oswego High School, my memories of lunchboxes came flooding back, courtesy of a colleague, and a pail-eontologist of sorts, Josh DeLorenzo. Josh is a social studies teacher—a darn good one—who was probably born a generation too late. His vast knowledge of everything '60s and '70s, from politics to pop culture, serves him well in front of his U.S. History classes. He brings his lunch to work everyday, not in a modern insulated vinyl lunch sack, but in a good old-fashioned metal lunch pail. The sound of him setting his lunchbox on the table, releasing the metal latches, and creaking open the lid, brought me back to metal lunchboxes that I owned, which my mom would pack with carbo-laden noontime meals of the 1960s—a PB & J sandwich (on white bread of course), chips, and Hostess cupcakes.

There's something about a metal lunchbox that brings back fond memories. Author Scott Bruce in his book *The Fifties and Sixties Lunch Box* writes, "The appeal of lunchboxes was emotional. Between birth and the brown bag, you weren't what you *drove*, but what you *carried*. Your net worth in the blackboard jungle was broadcast by that box dangling from your fingers. To many kids of the '60s, the lunchbox was an expression of who they were. Just as much as the foods that were transported to school in them, the lunchbox defined past generations."

DeLorenzo agrees. "Adults collect lunchboxes because of a connection to their youth. It screams nostalgia with a connection to a specific time and place in their lives," he said. I spoke with Josh in his classroom recently. On his desk was a metal Pac-Man pail, circa 1980, that he had carried from home that morning. He admitted that he's not a true pail-eontologist, but he does possess a small collection of lunchboxes just as a conversation piece. His modest collection does not include his most memorable childhood lunchbox, one depicting The Dragon's Layer.

I can only recall two lunchboxes I owned over the years before I was too cool for a lunchbox and graduated to the brown paper bag in seventh grade. I went searching for my grade school lunchboxes on eBay recently and found them both. I was certain of the color of the first, and

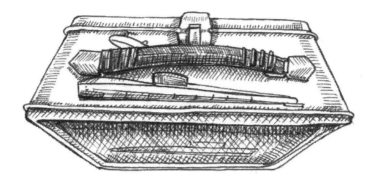

knew that it had submarines on the sides. My initial online search was centered on the TV program *Voyage to the Bottom of the Sea,* but the vintage lunchboxes I found for that show were much more colorful than my recollection of a sea-green colored pail with a red handle. Then I hit pay dirt. A generic search for "submarine lunch boxes" brought my '60s lunchbox back from the grave, in living color, on my computer monitor. Right before my eyes, appeared the USS Skipjack, Nautilus, Seawolf and other subs from the fleet, just as they were when I toted them to St. Paul's Academy everyday almost 50 years ago. It's odd that I don't recall a childhood fascination in subs (other than the edible type), and I'm positive I've never ridden in one. My guess is that the submarine lunchbox was the one on sale for $1.75 at the Green's back-to-school sale in 1963, so my mom bought it. (So much for the psychobabble I mentioned earlier about a lunchbox being an expression of who the child is!)

According to DeLorenzo, there's a lot more than nostalgia and Twinkies in metal lunch boxes. There's gold in some of them. Collecting these relics of a bygone era has become a big business. "Condition drives everything in collectibles, especially metal lunch boxes," he said. "Like old toys, nobody thought of them as collectible back then; they were functional."

He said the real marquee value lies where two different collectible worlds meet. "If there's a '60s *Star Trek* lunchbox that is rare and all original *Star Trek* memorabilia is rare, then the sky's the limit as far as pricing goes."

My other childhood lunch pail was easier to find on eBay, and seemed to illustrate Josh's point. It was an Alladin brand "Fess Parker as Daniel Boone" box from 1965. Current auction price—$350!

Whatever your most memorable lunch pail was, be it the Jetsons or the Munsters; Barbie or Mystery Date, as we've taken this stroll down memory lane, I'll ask you one final question that mom likely asked every morning on your way out to school: "Did you remember your lunchbox?"

•

Getting Our Kicks
(April 30, 2014)

I drove past an Oswego elementary school last week where a spirited game of recess kickball caught my eye.

That game of kickball did more than give a bunch of sixth graders a break from the rigors of their new Common Core lessons; it gave me a flashback to some of the best kickball games in history—those played in the St. Paul's Academy parking lot in 1971 during lunch hour.

If you went to Catholic school in the '60s and '70s, the lunch hour was truly sixty minutes long. At St. Paul's, the majority of students walked to school, so they had the luxury of going home for lunch, no doubt to hot soup and a sandwich prepared by their stay-at-home moms wearing aprons just like June Cleaver in *Leave it to Beaver* or Mrs. "C" in *Happy Days*.

But some of my classmates and I had to eat lunch at school either because we lived too far from S.P.A. (west-siders or kids who lived "in the country"), or we had working moms and dads. Anyway, after a quick lunch out of our metal lunch pails (no hot lunches were offered), we went outside to play.

I don't think we ever had adult lunch monitors or teacher-aids keeping an eye on us outdoors. Our lunch lady was a gentle, little old lady by the name of Mae Watts. I'm positive she collected milk money and watched over us while we ate in the old bowling alley-turned cafeteria on the first floor of St. Paul's, but I don't think she ever supervised us outside.

Kids today are lost without adult organizers and supervision, but that never seemed to be a problem for us. In the winter, we would slide down the hill behind the school or play "king of the hill" on the tallest snow bank we could find. But when the snow melted in the spring, the real pastime for us was kickball. It only took a red kickball and some hand-painted bases to occupy us "lunch kids" until afternoon class began.

If there was a kickball Hall of Fame, we'd all be charter members based on our accomplishments on that sliver of asphalt between the old St. Paul's Church and the school that's now called Trinity Catholic. With home plate facing the east and positioned about midway between the church and school, we had plenty of room to chase down kicked balls— with two exceptions.

One was when one of my classmates, maybe Jimmy Smegelsky or George Cuyler, would kick the ball onto the roof of the three-car garage adjacent to the school. It was a flat, unforgiving roof that gobbled up a lot of kickballs. Generally, a kick like that would end that day's game until one of our friendly custodians, Mr. Howard Vincent or Mr. George Paeno would retrieve the ball before the next day's lunch break.

The bigger problem was when someone like Burt Knight or Mark McGiff would really connect with a solid kick sending the ball sailing over all of the outfielders' heads. Unlike most of today's schoolyards, there was no fence enclosing ours. Too many times to count, we'd watch helplessly as a well-struck kick began rolling down East Sixth Street. Picture a red kickball gaining momentum down the steep East Sixth Street hill, with several Catholic school kids in pursuit, while the kicker

proudly pranced around the bases in a home run trot. These balls, pulled by gravity, gained even more speed as they rolled through the intersection of East Sixth and Oneida Streets. Our classmate Donnie Gill would often see our ball roll past his house at the foot of the hill on its way towards Bridge Street. If we were lucky, the ball would come to rest near the old east side fire station (now the Comic Shop) at Sixth and Bridge.

When the ball made it that far, as long as the outfielders were still in pursuit, they'd often cross Bridge Street to buy a well-deserved candy bar or bottle of pop at Carson's News before trudging back up the hill to resume the game. Sometimes, the next pitch would be rolled 15-20 minutes after the previous kick, but the game always went on.

The teams would eventually grow as our friends came back to school from their home-cooked lunches, but no worries—we evened up the teams and didn't skip a beat in the competition.

Times were different back then. We didn't need a trophy for our wins or parents bringing us Gatorade (heck, Gatorade wasn't even invented yet!) for hydration, and we didn't even need adult supervision. All we needed was our lunch hour, our friends, and one red kickball to make memories that have lasted a lifetime.

•

6

ROCKETS, TRAINS, AUTOMOBILES, & BIKES

Remembering Rail City

(July 24, 2013)

Summer is quickly fading, and it won't be long before school kids are writing the clichéd "What I Did Over Summer Vacation" composition. (Yes, they *still* do that.)

As a former teacher, I'm proud to say that I never asked my students to write that dreaded rite of autumn. I never made that assignment as an educator because I hated writing that topic when I was a kid. I think it was assigned every year of elementary and high school, and I even had a college professor resort to that old mainstay for an opening week writing piece one semester.

The reason I disliked writing that task is that my family rarely did anything exciting over the summer. While my classmates were writing stories about cross-country car trips to destinations like the Grand Canyon or Disneyland in California, my family took one small trip every summer. We'd pack dad's Pontiac Bonneville and head to Gananoque, Ontario, Canada. To my brother and me, the final destination wasn't the highlight of the trip, though we did get to swim in a pool and stay in a motel for one night! But the highlight of our vacation usually occurred before we ever left Oswego County. It was the annual stop we made at Rail City.

I was probably a little too young to appreciate the historical value of Rail City in the 1960s, but now, I'm too old *not to appreciate* what Stanley Groman did on 150 acres of land near Sandy Creek. Basically, Dr. Groman, a Syracuse physician, re-created a nineteenth century southwestern U.S. city in Oswego County, in the middle of the twentieth century. His city featured over a dozen steam locomotives, trolley cars, firefighting apparatus, and a classic water tower.

I visited what's left of Rail City on Route 3 the other day and spoke with Dr. Groman's son Bob. According to Bob, his dad was a visionary, a pioneer, a preservationist, but most of all, the ultimate "people person." The good doctor was apparently one part P.T. Barnum and one part Walt

Disney. His hobby-turned-obsession was costly, but you can't put a price tag on memories, including Bob Groman's and mine.

In addition to the booming steam engines and the piercing train whistles, my favorite recollections of Rail City were the re-enactments of train robberies that I recall as clearly as any childhood memory.

Tourists would be enjoying the mile-and-a-half ride in the countryside, through the darkened engine house, past Boot Hill

Cemetery, when a bandana-clad posse of train robbers on horseback, wielding guns, would appear out of nowhere and board the train to "rob" the passengers. I'm not sure what everyone else was thinking, but I wasn't going to hand over the quarters I had saved for the "magic fingers" bed massage at the Country Squire Motel in Gananoque, or my Mickey Mouse watch, to a band of marauders. After stealing the passengers' valuables, the villains would ride away with their loot and fire a couple shots from their Colt .45s—just to scare the daylights out of us. It worked on me! The first couple times I must have wondered why my dad didn't do something, like they did on the TV show *Gunsmoke*, but then again, the masked men did have guns, and I knew dad was no Marshall Matt Dillon.

After our ride, we would always climb the spiral staircase to the viewing area of the water tower, where, according to Bob Groman, on a clear day, you could get a great view of not only Sandy Pond, but Lake Ontario as well. Then we'd head to the general store to buy a Rail City souvenir. The elder Groman, always the promoter, stocked his general store gift shop with everything from bumper stickers to cowboy hats; from pocket knives to wall pennants.

When it opened in the summer of 1955, 30,000 people visited Rail City. Dr. Groman's passion endured until the mid '70s. Gradually, Rail City became smaller and smaller, like a locomotive pulling away from the station. In the 1990s, Rail City the *attraction*, became Rail City the *museum*. Artifacts and hundreds of photos were put on display. Interest in the museum waned as well, and now, only a solitary building remains where once eight or nine structures stood. But that remaining building, like its caretaker, Bob Groman, is a treasure trove of Rail City history and railroad memorabilia.

Bob, now retired himself, is charged with passing along what's left of his father's dream to a generation that only knows trains through the cartoonish *Thomas the Train* and *The Little Engine That Could*. He's hoping to find a proper home for what remains of the memorabilia of what was once a grand destination.

Since we can no longer get all aboard the historic Old #38 steam locomotive that once rumbled through Rail City, we can take a journey through history via the Rail City website (www.railcitymuseum.com) with dozens of vintage photos that Bob rescued from the scrap heap.

Surfing the web, however, is not nearly the same as riding the rails.

●

You Always Remember Your First (Car)
(March 5, 2014)

I was reading a car blog recently that said guys love their vehicles because the automobile provides a sense of freedom, power, adventure, and recognition in society.

I couldn't help but chuckle at this opinion as I reminisced about my first car—a 1971 AMC Hornet. Freedom? No. Power? None. Adventure? Yeah right. Recognition? Be serious.

The Hornet was supposedly a compact car in the same class as the Ford Maverick and Chevy Nova of the '70s, but those models seemed a lot cooler than my Hornet. Maybe it was the name. Whereas a Maverick made one think of the Wild West and the Nova conjured up images of space exploration, a Hornet was an annoying insect.

But despite this rather harsh assessment, I remember my first car fondly. Though it was manufactured with 10,000 other Hornets in the 1971 model year, I didn't buy mine until it had some wear-and-tear on it in 1976.

I think about my Green Hornet (that's what I called her, not because she was a crime-fighting superhero, but because she was both green and a Hornet) every time I run into long-time Oswego car salesman John Knosp. Everybody knows John or "Johnny" as my father called him. I spoke with John recently, and he figures that between 1961 and 1998 he sold about 7,500 cars in Oswego. That's impressive, but to me, Johnny will always be the guy who sold me my first car.

I remember the summer day my father and I trekked out to Big Ben Ford on Route 104 to go car shopping, just after our nation celebrated its bicentennial.

I needed my own car, especially since my father treated our family Pontiac Bonneville like a third son. Any question I began with "Dad, can I borrow the car to . . ." was abruptly interrupted with an emphatic "NO." Occasionally, I'd get an "I don't think so," and rarely a "We'll see" (which, of course, was just a euphemism for "NO").

So off I went with dad in search of my own sweet ride. There wasn't much on the lot in my price range (I had almost $1,000 saved). Moms have always steered teenage sons away from fast, dangerous cars, and dads of the '70s pointed their kids away from big gas-guzzlers. With those exclusions in mind, John pointed us towards a green, four-door, American Motors Corporation Hornet. At first, I wasn't impressed. The entire hood was rimmed in rust—not the kind of rust that will eventually flake off in pieces, but the kind of rust that was already making the engine visible in spots. When I sheepishly asked if there were any others to look at or test drive, Johnny said this was pretty much it. (Now, in retrospect, I have a hunch that my dad had orchestrated the entire "deal" ahead of time and my choice, really wasn't much of a choice at all.)

But a car is a car. When I see college students today driving brand new SUVs and 2014 imports, I laugh. Before I adopted the '71 Hornet, my buddies Jerry Brown and Sam Natoli drove me around for years in their beat up, but memorable, rides. Jerry had a 1964 Buick that we called "The Bomber." From piling some friends into the trunk to sneak into the drive-in, to burying it in a snow bank one New Year's Eve, it's probably a good thing that The Bomber isn't around to tell stories. Sam had a Skylark that we also had hundreds of adventures in; one of my favorites being cruising Bridge Street and having Dave "Agarn" Crisafulli imitating a siren out the window as heads turned and cars pulled over, assuming we were an emergency vehicle.

Though my car didn't have an adventurous side to her like my friends' vehicles, she served her purpose. It was a sensible four-door sedan that got me to campus, got me to my part-time job, and provided me some degree of independence.

I vowed to drive the Hornet into the ground while paying my

college tuition and saving money for the future, but something caused me to abandon her and look for a more stylish ride. In about 1978, my grandfather, who was still driving at the age of 89, got a new car—a Hornet. Suddenly, driving the same make and model car as my octogenarian grandfather wasn't cool. (It was especially embarrassing since grandpa's Hornet was in better condition than mine!)

Eventually I owned a couple Chevy Malibu Classics as a young, single guy before I moved into the station wagon and mini van phase of my life. But, as they say, you always remember your first (car, that is), and I do have mostly positive recollections of my Hornet, with one grateful thought—at least it wasn't an AMC Gremlin or Pacer!

•

3-2-1. Ignition. Blastoff!
(July 9, 2014)

When President Kennedy told a joint session of Congress in May of 1961 that America would put a man on the moon before the end of that decade, the space race was on, and all of America jumped on board.

Every segment of American culture became captivated by things related to outer space. Television debuted shows such as *My Favorite Martian, Lost in Space,* and of course, *Star Trek.* Detroit auto makers had already designed cars with rocket-like tail fins and named models after space objects like the Satellite and the Galaxie. The expansion baseball team in Houston was named the Astros and their home called The Astrodome. Even the Quaker Oats Company added a character from another galaxy named Quisp, who was often pictured on the popular breakfast cereal box with an outer-space ray gun!

NASA's Gemini program evolved into Apollo, and American families huddled around the lone living room TV set to watch flickering black and white images of blastoffs and splashdowns. My buddies were even more excited about the space race, because among our friends, was our own aviation expert, Randy Vincent.

Randy was only a couple years older than me, but his ability to build and fly things made him a cross between Orville Wright and Neil

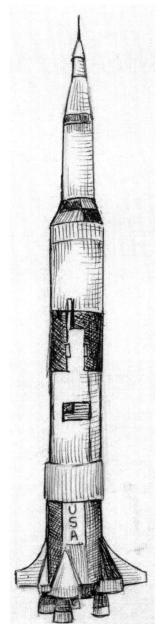

Armstrong to the rest of us boys in the neighborhood. I'm not sure how Randy got his initial interest in aviation, but last I heard, he transformed his childhood hobby into a career at aerospace giant Martin-Marietta—no surprise to any of us who knew him back in the day.

If Randy was the mission commander, the rest of us were the search-and-recovery team for his flying machines. Like the Navy frogmen who would jump into the ocean and open the hatch on NASA's manned space missions, my friends and I would jump on our bikes to follow a rocket or an untethered gas plane that had drifted off course.

We'd watch with fascination as Randy would prime his gas airplane engines with fuel, wind the propellers, and fly them around the park.

Our real vicarious thrills, though, came when Randy graduated from planes to Estes rockets. Word would spread like wildfire through the neighborhood when Randy came home from a trip downtown to Aero Sporting Goods with a new rocket kit. These rockets came in all sizes, and they captured the imaginations of the first generation of space age kids in Oswego's first ward.

The launch pad was usually centerfield of our ballpark, right across the street from Randy's Ontario Street home. The landing zone was a little harder to pinpoint, especially with the fickle winds of Lake Ontario. When those winds were favorable, a launch time was set, and just like Apollo 11, the countdown began. I'm not sure how the ignition process worked, but a large battery was involved, then a smoldering wick, and a few seconds later, the rocket would shoot into the air. When it reached a certain altitude, a parachute would deploy, allowing the main body of the rocket to float to earth—just like on TV. We'd often chase those rocket parts for blocks, and we'd sometimes even have to climb trees to retrieve them.

One of my most distinct memories of a launch (and I swear, I'm not making this up) was what we called the first "manned space flight" from the Diamond Match sandlot ballpark. I confirmed the details recently with Dave Smith, who lived two doors down from our rocket whiz, and we both recall the same details.

Most of the rockets Randy blasted off had small compartments in them, maybe for a plastic toy soldier, or a piece of paper like the old message in a bottle. One day, no doubt inspired by the Apollo moon missions, we decided to place a living creature in the passenger compartment. Though there were plenty of frogs in the tall grass at the park, we decided that we'd send a hamster into space. Just like NASA had done years before with a rhesus monkey, Randy launched the first rodent from Ontario Street into space.

The boys in the neighborhood were buzzing with excitement from the countdown, to the launch, and finally the retrieval. We weren't sure what we'd find when we opened the rocket's hatch after it returned to earth. Had the hamster fallen out? Was it burned to a crisp? Neither. It was still inside. I'm not sure if rodents can be traumatized or suffer from shock, but this hamster was shaking like a leaf.

Was it cruelty to animals? Probably, but no worse than burning bugs with a magnifying glass that was an occasional pastime for us kids on a sunny summer day. Boys will be boys.

The late '60s and early '70s were an exciting time for space exploration, whether the flights blasted off from Cape Canaveral in Florida or a launch pad on a patch of grass in Oswego, New York.

Come Along for the Ride

(May 1, 2013)

I love riding bicycles. I always have, and as long as my body holds out, I think I always will. Since May is National Bike-Riding Month, why not take a ride down memory lane with me.

There's just something special about riding a bike. To a kid of the 1960s, his bike was his independence, giving a twelve-year-old the same feeling of freedom that a driver's license would give the seventeen year-old several years later. When we weren't "walking to school in blizzards, uphill, both ways," kids of my era used bikes to get everywhere. We would ride to Little League practice and the corner store; to grandma's house and to church on Sundays.

I remember many of my bikes, and actually have old photos of me riding them. (One of my favorites is on the cover of this book.) What I remember most about my bikes was picking them out. I never received a bike for Christmas, probably because getting a bike in the middle of an Oswego winter, is a form of torture to a child. Try explaining this logic to a 7-year-old on Christmas morning: "Santa brought you a bike, but you can't ride it until the snow melts in five months!" My parents never taunted me like that.

Instead, when spring arrived, I remember going with mom and dad to the Western Auto store to pick out a bike. (I'm sure I had little tricycles and training-wheel bikes when I was very young, but this is the first one I remember picking out myself.) The bike I fell in love with had brighter red paint, and shinier chrome handle bars, than anything I had ever seen. I took great pleasure in just riding up and down my street, waiting for somebody to say "Wow, that's a cool bike."

After breaking-in my bike that first summer, I was ready for an upgrade. Obviously, bicycles were not like school shoes—you couldn't get new ones every year, so I decided to accessorize my bike. When I made out my Christmas wish list, I asked for the Vrroom Motor. This was the kind of noisy toy that kids loved and parents hated. Remember the Vrroom Motor? It was a Mattel product that would strap to your bicycle's frame, and powered by a couple D batteries, would make motorcycle noises. Not only did it sound neat, but it looked cool too. It made your bike look like a classic Indian motorcycle. It came with its own key and ignition. Nothing could make a bunch of seven year olds on bicycles sound more like the Hell's Angels than a few Vrroom Motors.

Of course, the predecessor to the Vrroom Motor was the baseball card, attached to the bike's frame with a clothespin so the spokes would engage it as you pedaled. It didn't quite simulate a motorcycle, but it did make a cool flapping sound. There are countless grown men today whose 401 K retirement accounts would be larger if they hadn't taken that Mickey Mantle rookie baseball card and clipped it to their bike for sound effects!

The baseball/bicycle connection can be taken a step further. What boy of the '60s didn't head to the park for a day of sandlot ball with his baseball mitt dangling from his handle bars, a ball jammed into the frame and a bat diagonally wedged in the handle bars?

To many former Oswego kids, a trip to the bike shop was a thrill. I was one of those kids. In addition to Western Auto, I distinctly recall buying bikes at Circle Supply on West First Street and Fenske's on West Second. I bought a lime green Huffy stingray, with a banana seat, at Circle Supply. I remember it being a little out of my parents' price range, so I had to "pay them back" with money I made taking out garbage cans on trash day at Sylvan Glen Apts.

The rows of Schwinns at Fenske's created a perfectly symmetrical rainbow the minute customers entered the store. I know they sold all kinds of household appliances at Fenske's, but they could've been selling real talking puppies, and I'm pretty sure no kid would've been distracted from the bicycles for sale. The last bike I bought as a teenager was a yellow 1973 Schwinn Continental ten speed. I am restoring this forty year-old relic, in my basement, and when I'm done, I plan to ride by 106 West Second Street where Fenske's was, just for old-time's sake.

Whatever seed was planted in my childhood about bicycles has stayed with me into adulthood. I'm not a bike racer and certainly not a tri-athlete, but I still love to ride my bike. Within the past few years, I have ridden my bike along the 1,000 Islands Parkway in Canada, over the Golden Gate Bridge in San Francisco, and down the Klondike Highway in Alaska, from the summit to the seacoast town of Skagway. But in spite of the beauty of each of these locations, my favorite biking memories are still from our Oswego.

•

Mike McCrobie

7

BEYOND OSWEGO

A Quazy Visitor from Outer Space
(April 3, 2013)

I'm not sure who first said that breakfast is the most important meal of the day, but I'm sure I never heard that saying as a kid growing up.

Knowing what I now know about nutrition, I'm surprised I didn't have a heart attack before I got my driver's permit. The breakfast foods of today are polar opposites of the artery-clogging morning meals of my childhood. Today, energy bars, Greek yogurt, and smoothie concoctions containing healthy ingredients like flaxseed have become all the rage, not only for the health-conscious baby boomers, but for young people as well.

My childhood breakfasts were anything but hale-and-hearty. My mom was 100% Irish, and God rest her soul, all the stereotypes and punch lines you hear about Irish cooks were true of my mom. Paula Deen, she was not. So, for weekday breakfasts, my brother and I were on our own. It was the hour between the time dad left for work, and the time mom woke up, so, being a chubby kid, I usually ate for the full hour. I ate cereal by the box. I figured that since my parents got their energy from hot coffee, I'd get mine from cold cereal—several bowls of sugary cereal, drenched in *whole* milk (skim was for wimps). If something looked or sounded like it was good for me, forget it. In fact, there might still be a box of Grape Nuts or Shredded Wheat hidden in our pantry on West Van Buren Street (even though we sold the family home in 1999)!

Captain Crunch, Tony the Tiger, Toucan Sam, and the Lucky the Leprechaun kept my brother and me company in the kitchen most mornings. That is, until a visitor from Planet Q in outer space landed on our breakfast table one day. His name was Quisp. I loved Quisp. His friendly rivalry with his Quaker Oats counterpart Quake, was played out on the back of cereal boxes and in cartoon television commercials for about a decade beginning in 1965, the height of my cereal-eating career.

After Russia began the space race with its launch of Sputnik in 1957, and JFK pledged to put a man on the moon by the end of the 1960s, America and Americans were obsessed with the space race.

Children's toys, finned automobiles, and even breakfast cereal producers like Quaker Oats Company, jumped on the outer-space theme. I ate so much of the saucer-shaped corn cereal, I almost expected to sprout antennae like Ray Walston's Uncle Martin from the *My Favorite Martian* TV show I used to watch.

I thought Quisp died a slow death sometime in the '70s, while I was distracted by typical teenage pursuits. Perhaps Quisp fell victim to Russian cosmonauts in some type of "quazy" space misadventure. But apparently, Quisp lives and still resurfaces in stores in various parts of the country every so often.

Memories of the past come flooding back when you least suspect them. That's why I was immediately transported back to the 1960s when I saw a display of Quisp recently at Paul's Big M.

I never studied business or marketing, but apparently there is something in the grocery industry called "guerilla displays." This is when stores buy a quantity of an obscure product or "niche merchandise" and sell it on a limited basis, only until the supply is gone. I have to admit, it didn't take the Big M long to sell out of Quisp in 2013, because when I saw the familiar blue box from the 1960s, it was as if I was jettisoned back to my parents' kitchen table by some type of way-back machine. I bought ten boxes, because I always get hungry taking a long trip down memory lane.

Say it Ain't So, Joe

(October 30, 2013)

Joining me in the ranks of the newly retired this year was a soccer star (David Beckham), a Hall of Fame baseball player (Mariano Rivera) and a Pope (Benedict). But there was another retirement that might have slipped under the radar. The news came out of New York, where the Topps Company announced the retirement of Bazooka Joe.

Every American who was born after World War I (and that's almost the entire current U.S. population), should know who Bazooka Joe is. He was born in an era when penny candy was less than one cent (yes, for a while, you could purchase two pieces of Bazooka bubble gum for a penny). Over the years, Bazooka bubble gum gradually evolved into one of our most iconic candies.

As a kid, a trip to our corner store for penny candy usually yielded about three or four pieces of Bazooka. The dividends inside the famous red, white, and blue wrapper were better than the interest rates on some of my current savings accounts. The way I looked at it, we got four things for our penny investment—the bubble gum, the comic, the fortune, and the merchandise offer.

By some scientific phenomenon, the gum was ridiculously hard until you popped a few pieces in your mouth. Then, it quickly softened, making it suitable for snapping loudly, or for blowing bubbles while passing time in right field as a Little Leaguer.

Though we paid for gum, the other fringe benefits were awesome. One of those fringes was the comic. They could've wrapped the piece of pink bubble gum in plain wax paper, but instead, the people at Topps introduced us to Bazooka Joe. The kid with eye patch taught us a lot about puns—bad puns. One after another, as my friends read the comics, the jokes would go over like lead balloons. But we read them anyway.

If the corny jokes made us groan, the fortunes on the comic gave us hope for the future. At various times, I'm pretty sure that Bazooka Joe fortunes predicted that I would become a lawyer, an architect, or a skin diver. Other predictions were more generic like, "What you think won't happen, *won't.*" Little did we realize as ten-year-olds, that a college philosophy professor a decade later would base an entire lesson on such cryptic quotes.

So we enjoyed the gum, a comic, and a fortune. But my favorite bonus that the little wax wrapper provided was a chance to send away for a "special offer." For a couple hundred Bazooka bubble gum wrappers, you could send away for lots of neat things like monogrammed rings, telescopes, and pocket knives. Yes, pocket knives! It's hard to believe, but a kid in 1968 could send away 55 cents and 5 Bazooka comics for a pocket knife that in today's world would get him detained by the TSA at an airport!

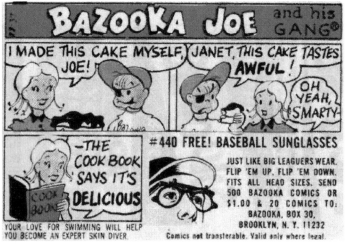

Bazooka Joe comic used courtesy of Topps Company, Inc.

One of the coolest things ever offered in a Bazooka comic lured me in the minute I saw it. I have a vivid memory of ordering a pair of baseball flip-down sunglasses—just like the pros wore back in the day. (Nowadays, of course, major league outfielders have $300 Oakley sunglasses perched on the brims of their hats when they lose fly balls in the sun.) But in the late '60s, for $1 and 20 Bazooka comics, I sent away for a pair of flip-down sunglasses. When they arrived, I couldn't wait to camp under a fly ball at the park and flip down the shades just like Ron

Swoboda, one of my favorite Mets' outfielders.

Of course, there were dangers associated with Bazooka bubble gum. One day, a group of us were bored with our usual summer pursuits, so we decided to have a bubble-blowing contest. With our mouths chocked full of Bazooka, we challenged each other to see who could blow the biggest bubble. (In my neighborhood, we competed at everything.) Needless to say, when the winner's bubble was popped, his face and some hair were covered in a pink shroud. Back then, you couldn't do a Google search on how to remove gum from your hair, so a pair of scissors and a self-haircut took care of the problem.

Fast-forward to 2013. The Bazooka of the past that was one part sweet treat, one part comic book, one part fortune cookie, and one part mail-order catalog has been rebranded for the modern era. You can still get Bazooka bubble gum, but it's certainly not a penny, and it doesn't taste nearly the same as it did back in the day. The comics have been replaced by brain teasers and activities with online links to the Internet.

Sadly, the fortunes, and the kid with the eye patch, Bazooka Joe, have been retired by the Topps Company.

Talk about bursting my bubble.

•

True Colors Come Shining Through
(March 19, 2014)

There are a lot of things I remember about the decades that some call the wonder years, and some of the interesting recollections are about the colors of the world in which we lived in the '60s and '70s.

I was brought into a black-and-white world when I was born in 1957. I have hundreds of pictures that attest to that fact. Whether it's a photo of our Christmas tree in 1962 or some family pictures of the Blizzard of '66, my early years were pretty much documented in black-and-white. A few people of that era may have been fortunate enough to have a color family portrait (often taken by the Olan Mills studio), but those color portraits were a luxury. My mom started filling our photo albums with color Kodachrome pictures, processed locally by either Bart Gentile or Frank Barbeau in their stores sometime later in the 1960s, just before she purchased a Polaroid instant color camera that actually spit out pictures that appeared right before our eyes!

Just as my kids, who were all born in the '80s, experienced the revolution from regular TV and movies to High Def and 3D, I lived through the transformation from a world televised in black-and-white to one documented in living color. I recall getting our first color console TV and being amazed at how good "Gilligan's Island" looked in color, and being horrified by the footage from the battlefields of Vietnam that Walter Cronkite brought into our living room each night on the *CBS Evening News.*

It wasn't the fact that we suddenly had color everything, but some of the colors themselves were memorable. One such recollection is about, of all things, household appliances. In today's culture, the desired appliances are the high-end stainless steel, but the colors of my youth were much different. I lived (and worked part time as a teenager) at Sylvan Glen Apartments. The Sylvan Glen complex is made up of seven buildings, 42 units in total. Every single one of those apartments had a dark copper-colored refrigerator and stove. Needless to say, when we moved into a home of our own when I was about thirteen, we also purchased a Hotpoint copper-colored refrigerator and stove. For a while, I thought that copper might be the only color they made '60s refrigerators in. I learned from visiting my grandparents, though, that they manufactured white appliances, but I realized the ones that they owned were holdovers from the 1950s. (Things lasted a lot longer back then.) But, lo and behold, when I started visiting friends' houses, I saw all kinds of colors of the '60s. Two of the most common stove and refrigerator colors of that decade were harvest gold and avocado green. Now those were colors.

Another color I reminisce about is blue. No, we never had a blue stove, lived in a blue house, or drove a blue car, but blue was the color of my grandmother's hair. Yes, gram was one of those "blue-haired ladies" of the '60s. I'm not sure what ever happened to all the blue-haired older ladies, but you don't see that look too much any more. Occasionally you'll see a high school kid at the mall with blue hair and wonder if a science experiment went bad or if he lost a bet, but the blue-haired women of the '60s have pretty much become colorful memories of the past.

There's another colorful fashion trend that is (hopefully) buried in the past forever. In this day and age, men's formal wear is generally designed in subdued colors. Today, the style for tuxedos seems to be leaning towards basic black, gray, or earth tones. But there are wedding photos and prom pictures somewhere, with guys of the '60s and '70s wearing hideous tuxedos in colors such as Lemon Chiffon Yellow, Sea Foam Green, and Robin's Egg Blue. What were we thinking? I know these photos exist because I possess some of them, in an undisclosed and heavily-guarded secret location.

Decorators must have knowledge of the hot colors of any given era, and the designers of the "new" Oswego High School were no exception. They had their fingers right on the pulse of trendy colors when the building opened in the fall of 1971. The 1,600 lockers were divided equally among four different colors. Some were blue (which makes sense, because blue and white have been our school colors for decades), but inexplicably, 400 of the lockers were an olive green, 400 were a sunshine-bright yellow, and the last 400, including mine, were orange—a shade I was reminded of recently when I had a drink at the bar of the same color at Vona's Restaurant.

There are other colors in the palette of my memory—from psychedelic tie dye worn by '60s hippies to the plaid uniform skirts sported by the girls at St. Paul's.

So I guess when people say Oswego has a colorful past, it's true in more ways than one.

•

Mike McCrobie

The Baseball/Radio Connection
(May 15, 2013)

First, it was *Newsweek* magazine. Then, *Daily Variety*, the bible of the entertainment industry, followed by four days of the *Post-Standard*, and the *MacMillen Collegiate Dictionary*. Each of these long-time print publications went the way of the dinosaur within the past six months with surprisingly little uproar or fanfare.

With iPhones and Kindles, and all sorts of tablets, the paper copies of many publications are fading like an Oswego sunset. But the Internet claimed another victim recently, when it was announced that the Syracuse Chiefs would no longer broadcast their games on the radio. Instead, all 144 Chiefs' games will be aired only on the Internet. Apparently, the Chiefs are on the cutting edge of this transformation, and may be one of the first Triple A baseball teams to broadcast solely on the 'net.

I'm sorry, but I don't have a smart phone, laptop, or a tablet, and I'll be darned if I'm going to sit inside on a beautiful summer night, at my computer, and listen to a Syracuse Chiefs' game.

I know I sound like a crotchety old (get-off-my-lawn) guy, but this is yet another American tradition lost to technology. Baseball has a long history on the radio. In the 1920s, games were broadcast by re-creating game action that was relayed via telegram, by using sound effects in studios. Sponsorships and commercialization increased as the medium did, but instead of succumbing to the emerging television industry, radio partnered with television by sharing on-air talent and resources. Now, each major league franchise has a radio flagship station to accompany its own cable television network.

I never minded getting sent to my room as a kid because of baseball on the radio. Through some stroke of good luck, my bedroom was at the highest point in our house on West Van Buren Street—giving me great radio reception from the little clock radio on my nightstand. The baseball gods were looking out for me.

144

Living in "Yankee Country," I could find the Yanks on several channels, but I grew up hating the Yankees. The Mets were my National League team, and any team that was playing against the Yankees, was my American League favorite. So, in the pre-Internet days of the 1960s, I was fortunate to get tremendous reception of station WBZ out of Boston. I would listen to the descriptions by Dick Stockton, Ned Martin, and Ken Coleman as they painted play-by-play images of Red Sox games in my mind that were every bit as vivid as today's HD televisions. Lying in bed, I could picture the Fenway landscape from the Green Monster to the Pesky Pole—and everything in between.

Likewise, I followed my beloved Miracle Mets of 1969 by tuning in Lindsey Nelson, Bob Murphy, and Ralph Kiner wherever I found them on the radio dial.

What former kid, who's now an AARP member, can't recall sneaking the transistor radio into school with an earpiece to listen to World Series games? My first such experience was in 1968. My father, also a die-hard Yankee hater, was a huge Detroit Tigers fan. In 1968, when I was in sixth grade, I tried the old transistor radio-in-the-desk-trick to listen to my dad's Tigers take on menacing Bob Gibson and the St. Louis Cardinals. Apparently, my teacher, Sister Josephine Claire, was not a baseball fan, nor did she understand that at age 11, I was able to multi-task by listening to the World Series and silently browse through *My Weekly Reader* at the same time!

Anyway, I made it home from school in time to see the final innings of game seven on TV on an October afternoon in 1968, while my transistor radio and earpiece were safely tucked away in Sister Josephine Claire's desk drawer—confiscated as exhibit A!

Lucky for us, the same Internet that seems to be dooming baseball on the radio has preserved some of the historical voices from radio's golden age. A quick Google search can yield an audio clip of Mel Allen's trademark "How 'bout that," or Vin Scully describing Sandy Koufax's 1965 perfect game. Another few clicks of the mouse and you can hear Russ Hodges at the microphone for Bobby Thomson's famous Shot Heard 'round the World when he declared, "The Giants win the pennant! The Giants win the pennant!" And that's not even mentioning Ernie Harwell and the often-imitated Harry Caray, who, for over fifty years each, called balls, strikes, and home runs on radio and TV.

So sometime this summer, whether you're driving in the car or sitting on your front porch, turn the radio on and find a ball game. It doesn't matter who's playing, what the score is, or who the announcers are, just enjoy the simplicity of the broadcast and the memories of a bygone era of baseball on the radio.

Note: The experiment of broadcasting local triple-A baseball only on the Internet was short-lived. With a change of leadership at the Syracuse Chiefs in 2014, games were once again on the airwaves instead of just on the 'net. All 144 Chiefs' games in 2014 were broadcast on 1260 AM The Score in the Syracuse market.

•

Happy Birthday Blockhead
(October 2, 2013)

An old and dear friend turns 63 years old today. But he's not just a friend of mine, but likely a friend of yours too. That friend of ours is Charlie Brown.

It's hard to believe, but Charlie Brown, the lovable loser who never did kick the football held by Lucy, has been eligible for social security for an entire year already. But the round-headed leader of the Peanuts gang (and spokesman for MetLife insurance) doesn't look much older today than when he made his debut on October 2, 1950.

If you're like me, you've grown up with Charlie Brown. In the past six decades, dozens, maybe hundreds, of cartoon characters have come and gone, but Charlie Brown and the Peanuts gang have endured.

Why? It's simple. There's so much to love about Charlie Brown. Different features of his make-up appeal to different aspects of our own personalities. My favorite image of Charlie Brown, and I've seen it drawn countless times by Peanuts creator Charles Schulz, is of Charlie standing on a baseball pitcher's mound. Whether surrounded by his teammates or upside-down as the result of a line drive hit back at him, Charlie the pitcher, is my favorite.

I think I like the Peanuts gang (and most comic strips for that matter) because of my own artistic shortcomings. My stick figure drawings don't even look like stick figures. I once drew a map of the United States on the blackboard while teaching *Huckleberry Finn* to a group of American Literature students. As I was finishing my masterpiece, a student raised his hand and inquired if Huck stopped at a farm on his trip down the Mississippi River. I said, "A *farm*? Why?" The boy said, "I figured he was at a farm because you just drew a cow on the board." When I explained that the illustration was a map of the U.S. and not a cow, the class erupted into laughter.

Due to my lack of artistic ability, I have always respected and appreciated those who could draw, and Charles Schulz could draw. But Schulz was not only a master artist, but the universal appeal of his characters comes from his deep understanding of the world, the human condition, unrequited love, child psychology, and so much more.

Besides Charlie on the pitcher's mound, there are so many other classic illustrations that have adorned greeting cards, t-shirts, and newspaper pages for decades. How about a forlorn Charlie Brown checking his mailbox on Valentine's Day with the thought balloon above his head saying, "Nothing echoes like an empty mailbox." Or a content Charlie, cuddling with his loyal beagle, Snoopy, with the caption, "Happiness is a warm puppy." I can't tell you how many times, as a child, I transferred these colorful images onto some fresh Silly Putty, from the comics page of my dad's Sunday newspaper.

For at least the past 25 years, the Peanuts gang is quoted annually in my house when we decorate for Christmas. I have a reputation in my family for picking a sparse Christmas tree. It's never tall enough or full enough for anyone's tastes, so not a December goes by without one of my kids or my wife paraphrasing Linus' famous line from *A Charlie Brown Christmas*, "It's really not such a bad little tree."

Of course, no American hero achieves greatness in isolation. He has to have a worthy supporting cast and the kind, gentle blockhead had one. From the sarcastic fussbudget Lucy, who dispensed psychiatric advice for five cents a dose, to her insecure little brother Linus, who innocently longed for The Great Pumpkin, the Peanuts Gang complemented Charlie perfectly. One of Charlie's friendly adversaries was even an inanimate object that he couldn't defeat—the kite-eating tree.

Though Charlie Brown was neither the most handsome nor the most popular boy in school, he did feel the angst of young love. Peppermint Patty affectionately called him "Chuck," but hid her true feelings, and the mysterious "Little Red-Haired Girl" was Charlie's unfulfilled romance. That's another reason people like Charlie Brown. Didn't we all have a "little red-haired girl" in our past? You know—that one childhood crush that never developed into a relationship, but you were left wondering "what if . . . ."

So here's a happy birthday to the loveable loser, the blockhead, a fellow AARP member and aging baby boomer, Charlie Brown on his sixty-third birthday!

•

ABOUT THE AUTHOR

Mike McCrobie, like his parents and grandparents before him, was born, raised, and educated in Oswego, New York. Prior to his retirement in 2012, he taught high school English for 33 years. As advisor of Oswego High School's award-winning student newspaper, *The Buccaneer Bulletin*, he was twice named Advisor of the Year by the Empire State School Press Association. He was also honored as a Teacher of Excellence in 1989 by the New York State English Council.

He and his wife Sally have four grown children, three of whom live in our Oswego.

He can be reached at ouroswego@gmail.com.

ABOUT THE ILLUSTRATOR

Melissa Francisco Martin was born and raised in upstate New York and currently lives in Fair Haven with her husband and two daughters. She is a published illustrator and graphic designer who has taught fine art and graphics at Oswego High School for over 25 years. Her students are recognized annually for their excellence in all forms of art in local, state, and national competitions.

Her interests outside of school include working on her century-old home and anything art-related.

She can be reached at mmartin@oswego.org.

Made in the USA
San Bernardino, CA
23 January 2017